Affinity

Affinity

◆

Managing Java Application Servers

John M. Hawkins

iUniverse, Inc.

New York Lincoln Shanghai

Affinity
Managing Java Application Servers

iUniverse books may be ordered through booksellers or by contacting:

iUniverse
2021 Pine Lake Road, Suite 100
Lincoln, NE 68512
www.iuniverse.com
1-800-Authors (1-800-288-4677)

Because of the dynamic nature of the Internet, any Web addresses or links contained in this book may have changed since publication and may no longer be valid.

The views expressed in this work are solely those of the author and do not necessarily reflect the views of the publisher, and the publisher hereby disclaims any responsibility for them.

ISBN: 978-0-595-45626-0 (pbk)
ISBN: 978-0-595-89927-2 (ebk)

Printed in the United States of America

Contents

PREFACE

To have an affinity for something or someone is to have a relationship or kinship. Affinity, as applied to technology, describes the relationship between the end user or client and the application server. The most common use of affinity applies to the load balancers that maintain the relationship between the client and the application. I chose *Affinity* as the title of this book to suggest that there is more than technology that keeps application servers running in today's enterprises. There is a much deeper relationship between the application server and the enterprise that must be in place to successfully run these complex business systems.

Java application servers are becoming the norm in business and, for the most part, are helping our enterprises to reduce their operating costs and improve efficiency. Integrating new technologies with companies' existing infrastructure can be challenging—the technologies and supporting applications are rapidly advancing, building seamless business applications that support the transition from the simple, composite applications of today to the service-oriented architectures of the future. I have had a great time supporting and building these systems and have great hopes for the technology and value-added benefits they bring to corporations.

As a technical consultant working with complex systems, it is my job to understand the life cycle of applications and what it takes to make them successful in a complex infrastructure. Working with these systems on a daily basis presents a number of challenges. This constantly keeps me thinking about the interdependencies among the technologies and how we use them to accomplish the business objectives of the customer. This book is designed as a practical guide to the challenges I have faced over the years. I hope that it will give you insight into what it takes to solve problems and build technically robust business applications. After reading this book, I also hope that you have a better understanding of the Java application server's role and how to better integrate it into the enterprise.

The goal of this book is to provide a practical view of what it takes to design support and build complex *n*-tier systems. While some of the principles and opinions are applicable across multiple Java application servers, most of my experience is with the BEA WebLogic server. The information offered here has strong relevance to the WebLogic server, but the issues and performance ideas are not unique to Java application servers. I believe many of the concepts can be applied to any system with which you are working in the enterprise. The inspiration for this book came from the many engineers who asked me to put my thoughts down on paper. It is difficult to cover every aspect of the Java application server, so I have selected the issues that I see most often when working with the application server. My goal is to give you an advantage when you build your *n*-tier applications based on Java application servers.

John M. Hawkins

affinity@ascertis.com

Intended Audience

This book was designed for anyone involved in implementing Java application servers. It will be most beneficial for application administrators, systems administrators, and IT managers who are looking for increased reliability of their WebLogic application servers. Having a good understanding of J2EE concepts, Java application servers, Web servers, operating systems, databases, and networks will help you understand some of the more technical sections of this book.

ACKNOWLEDGMENTS

First and foremost, I want to thank my wife and three beautiful daughters, Emily, Ashley, and Haley for granting me the opportunity to write this book. Writing a book takes a huge time commitment, and their willingness to sacrifice time with me so that I could commit time to this book made it possible. I appreciate all their continuing, daily support. I also want to give special thanks to my sister Mary, who encouraged me to write this book. I had been thinking about it for years but never found the time to sit down and write one. I also want to thank all the IT professionals who do the same type of work that I do and who have worked with systems and been through similar issues. While at times it seems like a thankless job that mostly goes unnoticed, I think our work is making a difference to the business we serve.

INTRODUCTION

It's near 6:00 AM, and you've been at the computer for the past ten hours. Nothing has gone right, and you know the project is behind schedule. You doze off for a second and then go back to work, knowing that you have to figure this out; people are depending on you. And then you start to think:

What am I doing here? This isn't my project. How did I get "volunteered" to work on this? How did I get roped into another enterprise production implementation?

Losing all track of time, you stare at the screen. The monitor looks blurry again, and you have completely drowned out the background noises. You remind yourself to focus, but you keep hearing laughter from the other room. While deep in thought and feeling somewhat dazed and confused, you feel a tap on your shoulder. You had completely forgotten that someone else was in the cubicle with you—it is the senior project manager, who says, "The director is on the phone. He wants to know if we are going to make the 6:00 AM milestone."

The 6:00 AM deadline definitely seemed feasible an hour ago and completely possible on the project plan, but now it's 5:50 AM, and you don't know how you're going to get out of this one.

You realize that you need to respond to the project manager, but you can think only about the issue and what you can do to fix it. So, after hours of being in a nearly catatonic state, your head dizzy from a mix of junk food and caffeine, you finally stand up.

A line of about twenty-five people are standing shoulder to shoulder in front of you. You wonder when they arrived.

You think, *I guess the party must be over. All of them look hungover and fighting off sleep.*

There is complete silence as you walk past the row of people. Someone might have asked a question, but you only remember saying that it doesn't look good. You realize that you are going to have to face the music on this one; the Web site belongs to a Fortune 100 company. If it doesn't start working soon, the company is going to lose millions of dollars.

You walk from one side of the building to the other with the senior project manager, ending up at a developer's desk. Upon arrival the director is waiting anxiously for you to arrive.

"Jack, is this going to make it? The vice president is looking for a status, and we are behind schedule. The whole site is freezing up when more than one user logs on. We are getting complaints from the business. The project managers want to roll this thing back."

You have been through this before and know that even if this were backed out, you still would run into the same problems the next ten times you tried to deploy this project to production. The team would push the production date a month out and would go through the same activity yet again. The company would not make the right decisions over the next few weeks, and you'd be right back in the same boat. So you tell him that you can fix the issues.

Feeling compelled to diffuse the situation, you start explaining the technical reasons behind the poor performance.

"The Web site is slow because all of the threads basically are doing the same thing. It looks like the application is having trouble getting information back from the database."

"Do we know why?" asks the IT director.

"A database call is started but sometimes never returned to the application. We have identified the database call and know it is an issue, but we don't know why it's slow."

"What do you need to do to fix it?"

You think of all the smart answers that you'd like to give. You would like to say, "I need to start the implementation during the day, not at midnight. I need some rest. I need to limit my days to eight hours, and above all, I need help from everyone before the night of the implementation. Furthermore, why am I here instead of the technical lead on the project? Why don't you have all the resources? Why is it just good enough to have me here?" But you contain your emotions. You know this won't fly, so you chicken out and say, "I need someone to look at the database call and tell me why it isn't working."

The director says, "How about Dave, the data architect?"

"If you can get hold of Dave at 6:15 AM on a Sunday morning, then let's get Dave." Then you think, *So, we have all the food, games, and movies for this implementation but no data architect.*

The director hands you his phone, and you dial Dave's number.

"Sorry to wake you, Dave," you say. "But I've got a problem, and I need your help to get it figured out." You explain the situation to him and send the offending database call. As an over-thought enterprise application, the database call had more characters than you can remember.

About ten minutes later, Dave calls back. He says, "I have the solution—the database query is referencing a table in the database that isn't used in the where clause."

We removed the table name at Dave's request and the query ran just fine with a low overhead.

This is the best news you could get, and you tell the development manager, "We only need a new build with the modified database query. Then we should be okay."

Within five minutes, the build is complete. You take the new code and deploy it to the production environment. All the application server instances are shut down and then brought back up. The quality assurance team is now able to log in. You make the modified 7:00 AM deadline with some time to spare—and get a quick rush of adrenaline. Because it is 7:00 AM and the nonpeak time for a Fortune 100 company's Web site, it does fairly well.

You finally go home to bed on Monday at 10:00 PM, after thirty-six hours of working at your computer, after receiving congratulations and thanks from the business. Now your wife is upset and feeling like you love your work more than her. There is no winner in this game. Over the course of the next few weeks, you find multiple other issues, resolve them, and have another enterprise implementation behind you.

The Internet has forever changed the way information systems work and that, in turn, has changed the way companies do business. The applications that are completely self-contained and don't have to communicate with other systems are becoming obsolete. The focus now is on the ability to integrate all the systems in the enterprise for a self-service approach to business. No longer does each system work independently. They are integrated and exchange information in a dynamic environment. Applications now are expected to bridge the internal computer systems with those on the Internet. The application server increasingly is becoming one of the popular components used to bridge the gap and allow applications to communicate with other systems. Application servers are becoming more and more sophisticated, allowing for building robust applications with less effort and a higher degree of success.

The vision is quite remarkable; imagine the ability to easily create enterprise applications in months or even weeks. Systems that would have taken years to complete fifteen years ago now take much less time. These applications work off of common frameworks that give enterprises the ability to create enterprise applications that can quickly scale to meet the needs of the business. The business finally is able to focus on the business requirements, rather than on the technology of getting the system built. It is a very exciting phenomenon and very rewarding to be a part of it. Satisfaction is very high, but it also can be frustrating at times when things go wrong. The challenge comes in trying to build and support these custom applications and then in putting them into a production environment, where they are accessed by thousands of users.

It is not the goal of this book to increase your knowledge on the technical specifications of the Java application servers—the specifications are always changing. Leave that to the application server developers; let them worry about meeting the specifications. You occasionally, however, will encounter a gray area. It's critical to understand the specifications, but in general, you do not need to worry about being an expert. Keep in mind that you control the areas in which you are going to specialize. A lot of that is luck, and the rest is your ability to get into the right place at the right time to build a deep understanding in an area.

The more time and money you are able to save for the company, the better your standing will be—and the more sleep you will get at night. Companies are able to save money—not to mention having their products and services readily available—when they open their business to the Internet. (Think back to just a few years ago—there was not a way to check your account balances online or pay a bill at 2:00 AM.) Companies appreciate contributors who can save money for them and reduce system downtime. Not everyone knows how to write and build a world-class application. The more you know about the process and the more success stories you can add to your résumé, the greater your odds of success. If you can find a way to implement the core concepts of this book, you will become more valuable as an employee.

The challenge you will face is how to get the company to adopt the changes from a grassroots level. It may start with just one application, but if you can solve the problems with one application and repeat the process, at some point, the systems will start to get better, and the organization will be more likely to support the process. Thousands of companies are looking for people with the ability to build and support their Java applications. The demand for these skills continues to increase and will for the foreseeable future. Once you know the basic areas on which you need to focus, you can research them as you encounter issues. You cannot become an expert overnight, but it is possible to become proficient in one of these areas—and maybe, in time, a guru. One of the success factors lies in knowing where to look when there is a problem, rather than focusing on one area that may not be at the root of the problem.

As a consultant, I have worked with virtually every component of an application server. I wrote this book to help you get a better understanding of some of the key areas that prevent these projects from being successful. I want to help you become aware of the common pitfalls, and I hope to show you how to better approach the challenges when you come across them. I tried to keep this book from being a technical how-to; rather, I offer a system that has proven successful for me with regard to building and supporting these enterprise applications. Even if you are part of an organization that does not support the process and is seemingly not interested in saving money, this book it still for you.

The most common Java application servers with which I have worked are BEA WebLogic, Oracle Application Server, IBM WebSphere, Sun Java System Application Server, and JBoss/Tomcat. Most of my experience has been with WebLogic, but each of these concepts is similar and can be applied to multiple application server technologies. The application server is considered as a commodity. So, to increase market share the vendors are selling application suites that run on their application servers, no matter which product or application is running on the server. However, the core components are the same. Java application servers have come a long way since they first came on the market.

Many companies ask themselves why move in this direction when the old way of doing things seemed to work well enough. The benefits of these technologies become clearer to me every day, as well as why the Java application server is so important for business. I hope it is clear for you, too. The more you immerse yourself in the technology, the faster you will become familiar with it and the more you will want to learn about it. I must tell you, though, that there is a learning curve that comes with the technology. Java application servers may be configured in a stand-alone mode in clusters, with or without a separate Web server. The business application (either written by a vendor, such as a CRM solution, or a custom code written specifically for your business) is then deployed. This book's focus is often on getting the code built and deployed. To my way of thinking, we live in a very exciting time. It is one of the best technologies I could hope to work with. I hope you enjoy the book and learn to appreciate the Java application servers as much as I have.

Layout of Book

Some parts of this book are very technical in nature. I do not expect everyone to understand all of the concepts, and in no way do I think that this book is a comprehensive look at all of the technical challenges you will run into while building applications on Java application servers. I will explore the process and offer a thumbnail sketch of some of the challenges you may run into when working with your Java application servers. I think that the most important way to start addressing the issues is to identify the tactical initiatives we need to get solved first. Once you have been through a session on getting the system to a more stable state, you can focus on the strategic initiatives. This will help you to drive and improve the process and, over time, get to the end goal of system stability and a robust repeatable process. Then you will see the results of all your hard work. I offer a little detail on what an application server is, but my assumption is that you already have had some exposure to the Java application server and are looking for insight into other components or what you can expect when taking an application from development to production. My main goal is to give hope to those who may be in the middle of a tough decision regarding their Java application servers and who need additional insight. I will share information that has helped me in the past. I hope you can learn from reading about my mistakes, rather than having to go through them yourself. This book is not so much a technical manual as a way to methodically approach the tactical objectives of getting applications up to expected standards.

I hope to identify the common areas that you should be thinking about when looking at your systems. I have taken all of my experiences in building high-performing systems and included the most important aspects that you need to consider when developing, building, and supporting these systems. Involvement in the process creates an equity stake for those participating. If there is apathy and a noncommittal attitude toward getting the issues fixed, then the problem most likely will become a self-fulfilling prophecy—the systems won't get any better. Even if you *could* fix all the problems overnight, until you change the process and start thinking about the issues before writing a line of code, you may end up back in the same situation next month. Taking it one step further, once you get the application back on track, the second step is to get the corporate culture in line with the transformation strategy.

THE CHALLENGES

Environmental Shifts

Companies are striving to cut costs, increase their efficiency, and gain additional market share by exposing their systems to the Internet. Business forces that change the way the business model works now require all of their different technologies to be integrated into one view. This is driving companies to upgrade and integrate their systems or lose the competitive edge. This is where the Java application server is able to add value. It is designed to integrate, to become the glue that holds the enterprise together. The Java application servers are quickly becoming the integration points for all other technologies and the platform of choice for net-new business applications. Requirements for the changes are coming so fast that for businesses to compete, they must develop applications in a matter of months that once took years. The challenge for companies that try to implement them is how to support the systems they currently have while expanding their inventory of new technology.

Business Transformation

In an effort to compete, there has been a shift from the traditional two-tier systems to the *n*-tier systems in the enterprise. A two-tier system is composed of two independently written programs that communicate with each other. Until recently, the two-tier was the most prevalent approach to designing and building business systems. It probably is still the most common. The *n*-tier has a subtle distinction—there is no requirement for the components to be installed or deployed on different hardware. Two examples of a two-tier application are printing a document and a point-of-sale system that gathers business data throughout the day and sends it back to the central server that aggregates data. An *n*-tier application is self-contained, like your online e-mail account. Now, technically, there is a client—the Web browser—but for all intents and purposes, the e-mail logic to receive, store, and send e-mail is self-contained on the server.

The *n*-tier application architectures give a tremendous advantage, such as economies of scale, for the enterprise systems. It also gives a tremendous advantage to the outside world. You can pass along the cost of data entry and many management processes to the consumer or business entity. The business is happy to save the money, and you are happy to have the business at a more affordable cost. It is a win-win situation. Getting to that state, however, is not a simple effort. The companies that adopt these technologies may undergo a rather turbulent shift while learning how to develop and support their new applications. In some cases, these shifts are so dramatic that companies find themselves with an outdated workforce that they need to retrain. At times, they will have duplicated the systems that they are maintaining during the transformation.

Companies that choose to revamp their systems have to make extremely difficult decisions in order to make the move. But making the change is important. It gives them the ability to compete in today's market. Making the shift to the new technologies gives the companies the flexibility they need to reach a worldwide market. So the question becomes not *do* we move to this new technology, but *how do* we move to it?

Good technologists who understand the technology can make the transformation go very smoothly. One challenge, however, is that with the newer technologies, there are not as many technologists who have a comprehensive understanding of how all the technologies work together. And even if you do get a good technologist, one may not be enough. The companies that try to transform and have bad experiences often drop these leading-edge programs in favor of a more simple approach to their information systems. And they may try this transition process multiple times before they are successful. Now, more than ever, businesses need to have a focused approach to developing and implementing these complex systems. The businesses that can handle the shifts are finding that they are better able to compete in this information-driven technological age.

With businesses becoming more dependent on application servers it is important to know what one is. An application server is a software engine that handles its own business logic and delivers services to a client. It is used for just about anything, from lead generation to customer relationship management (CRM), Web applications, and almost everything in between. Companies depend on these systems to be reliable for their mission-critical applications. The mission-critical applications are now available 24/7. In an online world, that requires companies to continually update and enhance these systems to keep up with the competition. Many of today's companies use the application server for their critical business needs, including large telecommunications companies, banks, trading firms, energy companies, finance companies, and many more. A minute of downtime may result in hundreds of thousands of unrecoverable dollars. In addition to dollars lost, the perception of the company may also be damaged. Customers expect to be able to log in and take care of business at all hours of the day. The challenge is in learning how to meet that expectation. If your company is unable to maintain its systems and provide the best experience for its customers, then another company certainly will be able to do so.

Organizational Challenges

How do you take a company that has been running for so long in a two-tier system and get it up to speed in an *n*-tier? For that matter, how do you take an existing brick-and-mortar company that finds itself losing market share and help it make the transition to a newly formed company with a competitive Web advantage? Making the transition to a company that has a strong presence and robust systems is not an easy task, but not making that transition will lead to lost revenue and profits for the company. Even if the company chooses to adopt the technology, it may fail, which wastes time and results in losing even more market share. Not only do we have to develop these systems, but they also must be as stable as possible. They must be able to meet business needs and may need to be developed with few or no defined requirements from the business owners. Ideally, when you build a system you would have concrete business requirements so that the company gets what it expects. In many cases, though, the need to compete for newly formed markets cuts down on your thinking time and puts you in survival mode. I have come in to projects where we must quickly adapt and start building before the requirements are in place.

Building and managing systems requires a strong commitment from senior management and determination from middle managers that they want to have systems that are stable and reliable and drive stakeholder value. However, if you do not have support from management; you can still make a difference. It will be up to you to drive the initiatives and do what you can to show progress. It is hard when you have groups of people who are fed up with the application that performs poorly. They may feel as if they have not been properly trained. They may feel that they do not know what they are doing. I know that they do not like being up at all hours of the night with these applications.

Consequences

If you cannot bring the systems to stability, you will most likely be replaced by someone who can. And if the company deems the system a commodity, the job will be outsourced to the lowest bidder. Large companies with deep pockets are marketing to the executives at your company. They say that they can solve the issues that you have not been able to solve. The choice, in my mind, is simple: you have to do what it takes to get the job done, and you have to make sure the job is right. Failure may be okay for some, for others failure is not an option. (For me, personally, failure is never an option.) And there is no reason to fail when implementing these systems. They may appear to be complex, but it really is a matter of better understanding the relationships or *affinity* among the different components. If you are committed to making the necessary changes to increase share value by providing reliable applications, then keep reading. I will define the steps it takes to get the application to a serviceable level. If you are in the middle of a painful implementation or have been part of a failed attempt in the past, you may think this is impossible. You are not alone; those who have had bad experiences also think this is a nearly impossible task. They are so used to the instability of the application that they believe that is how the application was designed. Blame is placed on the companies that built the products, the business owners, the vendors who sell the products, or anyone else they can think of. No matter who is to blame, the consequence for failure of the system is the same, jobs will be lost.

Production Changes Cost More

During the software development life cycle, the highest cost comes from making code changes after the application has made it to production. The earlier you can catch issues, the cheaper the cost of the software. Having requirement changes in the middle of development causes a huge impact on the budget. Not surprisingly, this is a big reason why projects go over budget and fall behind schedule. Large enterprises spend most of their time developing and designing software; they spend the least amount of time in getting it to production. They concentrate their dollars on what they feel is the core issue—getting the software written. Then they deploy the applications to production and, as a result, often have severe issues in production environments. Employees get frustrated and take on the attitude that they can own these issues and solve them or take the approach that it isn't their problem so someone else will fix it.

For the business application, code is written for the production environment. The challenge we face is that our environments and systems are built in development environments, with production as an afterthought. When a developer or architect does not understand the production domain, he must build to the domain that he does understand, development. Until there is an understanding of how these systems are used, along with the ramification of the design choices, the systems will not improve. It is important to have a good understanding of how the systems are going to be used before development begins. This will enable you to build the right solution and reduce the amount of production changes.

Vertical Teams Lack Breadth

Adding to the complexity, as companies get larger they departmentalize and focus their IT resources in one area or another. This means the production folks won't have any way to know about an application until it actually gets to production. The developers build most applications for development environments and have very little experience in production. This trend alone is creating technologists who are very specialized but have no common knowledge or background in how the system works as a whole. I find this to be the case more and more as I talk to customers. Everyone doesn't need to be an expert in every area, but having common knowledge on how all the system works together can make a difference to the overall success of the application. This vertical approach to building teams does have a number of advantages in the enterprise. There is the benefit of economies of scale when supporting multiple applications. Generally, there is a fairly decent knowledge-transition plan that must be in place to effectively support the process. The biggest deficit of this approach is that the engineers suffer the most. A number of new specialists do not have a clue of what is going on in the other environments. Yet more and more companies are adopting this model, which means fewer resources are focused on a particular product. This is the ultimate catch-22, trying to determine how to support infrastructure in a cost-effective way while maintaining a high level of technical proficiency.

Process Is an Afterthought

Businesses differentiate themselves by having unique products or services; a business's core strength is primarily about having a good process. This process helps define the company and gives the customers the experience they demand. A consistent process helps customers feel comfortable and keeps them coming back for more goods and services. Most of us are aware of this fact. We go back to those businesses that give us the highest levels of satisfaction. We expect the process to be identical to the last time we were there. That is what makes us repeat customers. Think about this the next time you visit your favorite coffee shop or burger stand. If your experience is not as good as it was on a previous visit, you feel let down.

For some companies, when it comes time to implement their IT systems, process seems to be an afterthought. The IT project they are working on is just one of many objectives. The project takes on a life of its own, and the main focus is on getting the code developed to meet the business requirements. Time-to-market becomes the goal, no matter what the cost. The challenge is that while there is a mandate to develop these systems to meet the requirements of the company, there is not a process in place. If there is a system, it is most likely flawed in one way or another, and that causes frustration and a feeling of losing control. The more complex, with more integration points the new system has will require a higher degree of coordination and planning to implement. When it comes to implementing these systems, you will find the undefined process makes implementation difficult. Companies seem to want to have systems in place quickly, and the process to do so is an afterthought. This may be the right philosophy. They are, after all, a service or product company, not a software company. So, when we develop these complex systems, there is even a greater need to have the process defined and in place, prior to gathering a business requirement or writing the first line of code.

Which Process?

I have visited and worked at companies that have had one or more process issues that should be addressed. There are only so many processes that you can adopt and keep in place when building a system. If you followed every process, every time, you might never get the system developed. This leads to questions going unanswered until the application may be in production—or close to it. Once the systems are in production, there is a limited knowledge-transition plan. How will we support the system, and what do we do when there is a problem? These issues are easy to put into the process and yet, time and time again, they are missed. Is there a knowledge base related to all of the issues that were encountered while developing this application? What troubleshooting methodologies are in place? Are the right people working on these issues? These questions—and more—may go unanswered when the application finally makes it into the production environment. In fairness to these businesses, it's not as if we're developing rockets to send to the moon or a safety restraint for a child's car seat. These are, after all, business applications that we use to improve the business process.

Build versus Buy

A custom business application offers all the functionality you choose to build and all the challenges of off-the-shelf packaged software in terms of the software development life cycle. You can build software that is custom-tailored to your business process. The integration may be easier than trying to customize an off-the-shelf product to fit your business needs. The advantage of building it yourself is that you will get the application you want with the look, feel, and integration points you choose.

The off-the-shelf product has a standard set of features that has proven successful in other environments. It has a process in place to build and deploy its software. The product is most likely very specialized to meet a business objective making integration with your business process more complex. There may be a great deal of mapping between the off-the-shelf product and your current business model. There are most likely standard support and bug-fix procedures in place. The off-the-shelf packages also may provide you with references of customers that have similar implementations as yours.

When you choose to build your own application, you take on all the responsibilities of the off-the-shelf company. Some of the groups you may need to support this process are a product management group, development, and QA (quality assurance) support, each under their own leadership. With the homegrown solutions the IT department takes on the ownership of the full software development life cycle for the application. It controls the applications' logic, which hardware to use, the database schemas to deploy and in what technology you will build the application. The more complex you make the system, the greater number of variables required to deliver this application. The more variables you have in your application the more resources and bigger need to have a plan in place to support the application. This all makes a large impact in getting your applications and environments ready for production.

Now that you have ownership of all the areas that need to be developed in the application, add the complexity of defining the business process and a nearly impossible schedule, and the task of successfully building and supporting the application becomes even more daunting. Companies compensate for it by solving the same code challenges, multiple times in each department, and each in a slightly different way. There needs to be consistency when you start developing code for your environments. Identify the shared components to the applications, enforce your development standards, and do the peer reviews and code reviews of the systems.

There are advantages and disadvantages when deciding to build versus buy. The more off-the-shelf applications you try to integrate and support, the more complex the environment will become and the higher your maintenance cost for these applications will be. Whether you choose to build or buy your software, as long as they are both deployed on a Java application server the concepts detailed in this book should apply.

Buy More Hardware

A common approach to solving performance problems and meeting capacity demands is to buy more hardware. The thinking is that one application server can handle one hundred users. If you need to service five thousand concurrent users, then you should have fifty instances to support all of the users. This might be the case, but you should know for sure before making a big investment, and you may still have the same issue you had prior to getting additional hardware. Purchasing more hardware may solve the immediate business need to keep the systems running, but it isn't the long-term solution to the challenges you face. The hardware is expensive to purchase and maintain. There are issues with adding capacity to the data centers and increased management cost to handle all the new servers, not to mention the licensing costs associated with the purchase. You must understand the application in its current architectural state with the settings as they are today. Understand what the implications are when you add more resources. Get a handle on your system before you start purchasing more hardware. This is not to say that you never will need any hardware and will use one machine for all applications, but there may be inefficiencies in your code. No matter how many servers you add, you will still have issues.

In fact, in one case an architect solved a capacity issue by limiting the number of concurrent requests the server could run. He set the limit to two concurrent users. In this current design, how many instances do you think he needed to meet the demand of 480 concurrent requests? The system would have required 240 servers to run with that architecture. I had a one-on-one meeting with the CEO, and he said that he was spending ten million dollars a month on hardware. There was a far more efficient way to solve the performance issues this application was having—it took about three days—but when I was done they were able to handle the capacity they needed with only twenty servers, not 240. How much money do you think it would have cost the company to go with 240 servers?

Hire More Employees

The same truism about adding more servers can be applied when it comes to hiring employees. Some companies believe that hiring more employees will fix the issues. You can hire as many people as you want, but if you do not have the right technical leadership, you are destined for failure. If you don't have a process in place that guides the company to successfully manage the systems, your shop will be a revolving door. I see this happen all the time; it's a waste of resources. When you add new people, you will be trying to jump-start newly hired recruits to get up to speed quickly. The work environment will become very stressful and employee morale may be affected negatively. Solutions are developed to solve challenges, and when those solutions are not implemented people may get frustrated and quit. The process is not in place to support the work that needs to be done. The continual practice of not listening to those who are trying to make the process better builds an apathetic view toward the systems and their stability. It ultimately creates a negative view toward the organizational culture. Individuals with domain knowledge may quit when they get frustrated with the issues and lack of stability of the systems. You can cut your liabilities by getting the systems stable, which improves employee morale and supports your employee retention plans.

Return on Investment

A business is valued in the market based on how it performs financially. Management can look at the average cost for an employee and compare that to their peers. If all things are equal, then you will have the competitive edge over your competition if you can keep your costs under that of your competition. The flaw in this thinking is that not all technical folks are equal, and depending on the mix of talent in your company, the productivity can change from group to group. You may be above the curve for cost per unit of work, yet your workers are ten times more productive than a similar company who is below the average cost per employee model. When you are trying to fit into the cost model and add the additional resources you are focusing on the metrics rather than efficiencies of operation. The metrics are showing that you need additional resources when what you really need is to become more effective. Thinking you are on the way to solve the problem you may have actually compounded them. You have now added overhead to your organization, with hardware licenses and desks for the new employees. It may result in a large organization that has only a few highly effective employees. This increases the likelihood that you will need to downsize your employee ranks or outsource your jobs to someone who can solve your problems. And this will be increasingly evident by the amount of work you are able to produce with the number of resources you have. The senior management level at most companies watches the numbers very closely. If you are unable to produce within the industry averages, then changes will be made.

When All Else Fails, Kill It

Java application servers, if configured correctly, should never have to be killed or shut down frequently to resolve performance issues. Java application servers have issues for a reason. The key is in knowing how to approach the servers from a tactical perspective, which will lead you to a more stable and more robust system. You might be surprised that a troubled application can be fixed relatively easily without having to make too many code modifications or fixes. The worst system I worked on had fifty percent availability. Each of the Java Virtual Machines was recycled at least once every fifteen minutes. It took some time, but I got the system from 50 percent availability to over 98 percent availability by adopting a definitive process for identification and resolution of issues. Recycling your application alleviates the immediate issue but does not fix persistent problems. If you have to recycle frequently, there is a systemic problem at the root of the issues. There may be more than just one problem causing the outages in the system. Understand that if something doesn't feel right, then it probably isn't. Kicking customers off of a system to clear up code issue is not acceptable if you are trying to run a for-profit business—or for any business, for that matter.

It will take time to adapt the process changes that solve availability issues; but to be successful you must put them in place. With the right process in place, over time, you can incrementally gain an upper hand by defining a winning strategy to bring stability to your application servers and the business they are trying to support.

Complexity

The companies that use application servers range from small businesses to large Fortune 100 enterprises. The issues related to complexity are mostly found in large corporations, but can apply to the smaller companies as well. The risk of an overly complex system is magnified when yours is a small company. Some companies market only one product, and their entire existence depends on the success of the application they have deployed in production. An unstable or complex system can drain resources in a small company and put the whole shop out of business. Regardless of whether you have one application or five hundred applications, the problems are similar; problems in a large company are just magnified by the number of applications.

When it comes to the business application that is built and deployed on application servers the more complex the solution the harder it will be to support. Keep your application architecture simple. Use frameworks to build the custom application and keep applications simple. There are always multiple ways to solve a problem. In some cases, each developer will choose to solve it a little differently. Extremely complex problems can result if there is not a clearly defined, common approach to solving architectural challenges. This also will lead to word-of-mouth or tribal transition of source knowledge about the applications. The larger the projects, the more complex the systems are and the more complex the challenges are. Large companies need to have strong technical leadership that drives the best practices and a structured approach to developing applications.

Common Approach

Regardless of whether you are a large company or a smaller company, the Java components you use or are going to use may be the same. The difference is the amount of times that you need to use them and the amount of integration between the dependent systems. Large or small, you can implement all the technologies, including SOA(service-oriented architecture). Some of the common components you may deal with are Web services, Java Message Service (JMS), Enterprise JavaBeans (EJB), Java Mail, J2EE connectors, and any number of other components. Depending on how you architect the solution, these components can be delivered in two-tier architecture or *n*-tier. In the enterprise, multiple architects may be designing different applications. It all depends on what new design the architect read about last week and whether or not they want to try it out as well as which direction they feel the application is going. It is important to have a common, consistent implementation when building your applications. Where does your domain knowledge reside? Do you keep that knowledge in the architectural units? Does this knowledge belong in the production arena? Production folks may be required to support these applications long term. When the knowledge is kept among the development teams or architectural teams, they become key players in the success of the project. Now that they are key players, they also are locked into supporting this application until the knowledge transfers to another unit.

Documentation

A key to having a supportable environment is to track and document the issues that are faced on a regular basis, from the first day of development to the production rollout and beyond. The little "gotchas" that are learned from the first day with the proof-of-concept to deployment, are the same ones that engineers will encounter years into the project. Successful projects have a good document trail that defines the issues encountered during all stages of the software-development life cycle, including the planning, architecture, proof-of-concept, development, and production implementation. For the average project, unless a process is adopted that forces the documentation and tracking of issues, the documentation is primarily tribal in nature if at all. The longer the project goes on in this state, the harder it will become to support and transition. The impact to engineers who are tightly coupled with the project is that unless they document and have a good transition plan, they may forever be tied to the project. This, in turn, will limit your growth and keep you from moving on to other departments. Even worse, if you abruptly leave the company without a transition plan in place it may negatively impact your future employment at other companies.

Tribal Knowledge

Tribal knowledge can be a detriment to any team, regardless of size. Tribal knowledge occurs when small groups of people become domain experts in the areas on which they are focusing. They become experts because they have been the only group working on these applications or components. They primarily have communicated via word of mouth and e-mail, and there isn't a concrete document trail to follow. The problem with this type of communication is that to understand their process and procedure, you must become a tribe member. Becoming a tribe member means undergoing a time-consuming indoctrination process to get you up to speed on the ins and outs of the system. The tribal system is the simplest process in which to transition knowledge, but it's the hardest system in which to get knowledge out of. That is why keeping your systems knowledge on a tribal system is bad for the company and hard on everyone. To determine if tribal knowledge is in use, ask any of the team members a question about a specific piece of functionality. If he refers you to the group who owns this functionality, this is your first clue they are using tribal knowledge. The second clue is when you are directed to the same person over and over again, and there is no one else in the group that can help. The third and final clue is when there is no process documentation for the answer once you get it. When only one person understands the information, you have a real problem, even if this one person is extremely helpful if you need to get an issue fixed. The question for management and others, however, is, "Why do we have an entire team to support this process when only one person understands it?"

Tribal knowledge becomes extremely dangerous when you have a conflict between two tribes—it can cause a complete breakdown in communication, and these breakdowns in communication continue for months—sometimes years. It may reach the point where the person with the domain knowledge becomes even more guarded with their information. The team of engineers handling the mundane tasks leave at the end of the shift and have a fairly easy job, while the tribal leader on the other hand is off fighting fires and solving all the application inquiries. Managers, project managers, and team members have given up on the team, but as long as the domain expert is kept happy, everything is okay.

When confronted by management, those participating in the tribal transition will give you a wide range of excuses as to why they don't understand the system—"I wasn't given the opportunity" or "It isn't fair that I didn't get all the opportunities that the other person got." Now you are in trouble: you may have a team that is supposed to be saving the company money, but they are mired in conflict and trying to determine who they can blame.

Truthfully, everyone is to blame; people need and want direction. Not everyone has the ability to create a vision when sitting in a department, nor is it their job. There is a certain sense of security when someone comes up with a vision that gives a clear path toward success. If you do not have that leader in your group, then management must find a way to create that vision for the employees of the team. We all have goals in life, but many of us do not have a clear vision of how to reach them. When we do not meet our goals and reap rewards, we may feel like failures.

Manual Process

I have worked on teams where only a small percentage of the team actively contributed; the rest of the team performed manual tasks that could have been automated. I see situations where a few team members determine how to do the work and the rest simply repeat the process. Part of the reason for using technology is to help with the mundane and somewhat mindless tasks. If you automate these tasks, you can save a great deal of time, and that time saved could be used for other, more productive activities. For example, if someone writes an application that monitors and recycles the application for an initial investment of $1,000 of development time and no maintenance cost, how much money is saved by not hiring a full-time employee to start and stop the application? The answer is simple. It is the cost of the employee's salary minus the cost of the script. The time it takes to start and stop the servers, as well as monitor the servers all day long, really starts to add up. Why would you pay for a full-time employee when you can automate the process? Even outsourcing would not be as inexpensive, because the automated script can do the work for you. More importantly, the scripts that person wrote become a primitive form of documentation—you can go back through the script to understand how it works.

Give Up

Companies tend to be cautious about adopting a new technology because they fear failure and think the application will be too complicated. For those companies that have failed at implementing their Java application servers, the only choice is to give up and return to what they know. Unless they are guaranteed to save money from a business perspective, they do not know if this system will help or hurt the bottom line; they are going to consider the applications ROI(return on investment). A properly designed application that reduces transaction costs and saves the company money is an asset to the business. If your systems are in a constant state of flux, you will not know from one day to another how they are going to perform. By not fixing the issues you are impacting the ROI for the business and are seen as a liability. The best option may be to go back to what you understand. There are some companies that really shouldn't have a high investment in technology—either they are interested in remaining small or there would be no lower cost with economies of scale.

Outsource

When a company considers outsourcing of an existing application, it is usually a long time coming, and in some cases, management can't be faulted for this decision. If you have an internal IT department, but you choose to outsource the development of your applications, it's generally because you either don't have confidence in your internal teams or that the cost of the application would be more than the cost of getting in the market. The outsourcing usually isn't a personal decision; it's a business one. If you look under the hood, you'll see that the culprit is poor financial performance. If you can get a high-performance application by outsourcing, then do it. You also may decide to outsource an application when you don't have the in-house ability to build or support this application. The issue generally does not relate to the quality of employees. There are some situations that warrant placing blame on the employees. I would suggest that the issue is more deeply rooted in the organizational culture and its inability to effectively deliver applications and first-class support. With outsourcing, you want to get a better process in place, one that you believe will be better able to deliver the results you expect.

THE SOLUTION

I've discussed some of the challenges that companies are facing today when changing technology and when just trying to keep up with their competitors seems insurmountable. The first thing to understand is that these systems weren't built overnight. The problems weren't created overnight either, and it takes time to make all the necessary changes. The longer it takes to get a sound strategy in place, the more confusing the application landscape can become. I once met an architect who said that it didn't matter in what the application components were written—if he had a Java developer. He insisted, he would have that component written in Java; if not, he would let the developer write the application in whatever language the developer knew. Just think about the problems he created for the company! Such a strategy allows the corporate landscape to dictate what the applications will look like. At some point you need to take a side and say, "This is how we build out systems." This is a challenge but if you want to build successful business applications, there needs to be a consistent approach.

Getting the applications back on track will take time—it takes time to know if you are successful. For each action you may not know the consequences of your changes for months afterward. The question is whether you have the time to wait—usually three- to six-month increments—to see if your changes are having an effect. What benchmark metrics do you use to see if you are taking the company further ahead or causing more problems?

Solvable

The truth of the matter is that these challenges are solvable. There is a technical reason why the systems function the way they do. The biggest challenge is to get a process in place to tackle the issues, one by one, until at some point you stop getting the late-night calls, and the systems start to become more stable. The second step is to change your process so that it includes the best practices in your development life cycle, which will help avoid these problems in the future. The more stability you bring into the environment, the more time you will have to focus on solving the IT challenges that will give the company the biggest return on investment. Changing how your systems work isn't a straightforward process; it may vary from company to company.

If you cannot think of a solution the solution will find you. It may be a mandate from above, or it could be just time for a change. I suspect that if you were to talk to your employees and coworkers, many would agree that it is time for a change—they just don't know what that change is. Think back to some of the challenges you faced most recently. Is there a pattern to these challenges? Do people complain about the same issues over and over again? To solve the problems faced in the company, each team member may choose a different way to fix the issue—one may leave the department, get promoted, quit the company, or open that coffee shop in North Carolina he has always wanted. There is always a downside to letting things continue down the wrong path, and the biggest downside is that if you don't find a way to change, someone else will find it. The path that person chooses may not be in the company's best interest. Some people may want to get as far away from a problem as possible, but the rest need to learn how to adapt to change. They need to focus on how to solve the problems, rather than how to escape them. I think there is a far greater sense of accomplishment when we tackle problems head-on. Keep a positive attitude, these problems have solutions, and over time, you can shift from survival mode to growth mode—growth that can continue indefinitely as your company's goals and aspirations grow.

Lay the Technical Foundation

Building your technical systems requires a technical commitment to the projects and issues at hand; moreover, it sometimes is more important to show the support of the issues than to solve any single technical problem. The solutions to the problem are available at your fingertips; the challenge is to get people in the right mind-set to find them. Doing this requires that technical issues be resolved so there is some breathing room to focus on operational excellence. To be successful, there must be technical initiatives that help reduce the amount of downtime in the environments. You may need to limit the number of projects in scope. Show the company that you are making the commitment by putting in the technical foundation to support the efforts. Systems today are so intertwined with multiple dependencies that it may be difficult to differentiate the root cause of a problem. The answer to technical solution may be found anywhere in the network infrastructure or dependent application and involves the various layers to include the networking enterprise server and, in some cases, the client's desktop.

Understanding the problem can be difficult in itself, but if we lay a supportive technical foundation to fix these issues we improve our changes of success.

Understand the Fundamentals

Working with any technology or any specialization requires an understanding of the fundamentals—a common knowledge base from which you can build. Before you can start to solve a problem, you first must understand the problem—and then understand why there *is* a problem. If you have identified the problem but don't understand it, you limit your chance for success. Understanding the fundamentals of systems—and *n*-tier systems, for that matter—is at the core of being able to fix the challenges in the enterprise. Once you have a firm understanding of the fundamentals that make up the framework of an enterprise application, you can get a more focused look at the technologies behind them. Understanding fundamentals is a key element to successfully identifying issues with your applications. The great thing about understanding the fundamentals for n-tier applications is they are not technology dependent—if you understand the fundamental problem, it doesn't matter in what the application code is written; the root cause is the same. By understanding the fundamentals, you will be able to solve not only Java application server issues but also any other issue that occurs in an *n*-tier architecture.

Think about the Process

By adding process into the system, you build confidence in those working with the systems (or tangent to them). Predictable outcomes are in line with the expected result. Process comes over time and through many iterations of working through issues. The process can be applied to your development teams, applications support teams, database teams, business analyst, and any other team with which you interface. The key to having good process is to have consistency among the various groups or departments in an organization. There are, however, signs of poor process in companies all the time. For example, Joe wants to leave his department for another. The work may be the same, the management the same, but the process is different. The team that Joe wants to join does things differently—it is more successful at working through the process. The accolades for this success go to the manager or team leader. But assuming all things are equal, why does Joe feel so compelled to change departments? You may have felt this way at some point, thinking about your personal benefit by moving to the new team. Did those team members make more money? Or was your desire for a change due to something deeper? Maybe you liked the manager of that team more than your own manager, but really, what is different from one manager to another? They all pretty much do the same thing, right? Or do they each have their own process that they are following? The process can be in how a certain manager manages you—these are intangibles, such as whether he greets you in the morning or smiles at some point during the day. The manager's operation can be quantified in a process. At some level, I think we all like to have process in our lives, process that brings repeatable results and with repeatable, successful results. A manager who is successful usually follows a different process than those who are unsuccessful. From the employer's perspective, a manager must drive consistency and process into how he interacts with employees. If he waits for a global vision from corporate, he may be waiting a long time. I think it is better to act sooner rather than later—take ownership of the process.

Build Your Documentation Plan

Documentation appears to be last on everyone's list of what needs to be done before production deployment. There are a couple of reasons for this: First, even if you spend the time writing the documentation, most people will not read it. Second, once you write the documentation, it is outdated the minute you make a change. The common practice it to get at least something done and document later. Documentation does not have to be in the form of a formal document. I think it can be advantageous to modularize the documentation into short, concise bullet points. Building your knowledge base of issues is how to start building knowledge transition, and it can be as simple as putting error messages in a text document and putting it on a share somewhere—that is better than no documentation at all; plus, it provides a log of what you have fixed with the system. Over time, you may go back to that log file and decide that you really didn't need to be so specific or realize that you now know what it means. Regardless, I think that keeping that log is invaluable both to you and to the company. You must do some documentation: at minimum, you must have a comprehensive implementation plan that contains all the steps required to create and deploy this application. Some of these plans are very detailed, and depending on how big the system is, this is a good thing. The plan should be created when you first push the code to the integration environments. As you find omissions with the plan, they must be updated in a timely manner. The more times you review and update, the more comprehensive and complete the plan will be. Keep the implementation plan as straightforward and simple as possible. The more complex it is, the more intimidating it will be—and the less likely it will be that someone will use it.

Manage the Environment

An environment team or the role of managing your environments needs to be a repeatable build process for the application that ensures consistent results are delivered every time you push code to a new environment. How you develop the application has a direct impact on the simplicity of the build promotion. Are you going to build out your environment automatically? Do you need to have the servers built out automatically, or can someone build them by hand each time? There isn't one best way to do this. The more complex the environments get and the more there is at stake, the more important it becomes to find a way to automate the process. If you try to build the environments by hand each time, there are likely to be mistakes (after all, humans are prone to making mistakes). A program, on the other hand, only makes the mistake you program into it, and you should be ready to handle those exceptions. There must be a clearly defined way to deliver application components to your environments. This process should also work in conjunction with the build process to make sure that you have delivered the correct build to the environment. There isn't one best way to go about doing this, and especially when you are trying to manage multiple technologies. In addition to getting the right build to the environment, it is also critical to get the correct configuration from a domain and property file to the environment. Part of the advantage of the Java application server is that you can reduce the amount of code that needs to be written. You still need to configure the application server in a number of ways to get the optimal performance. All of this must be tracked and documented so that when you need to build out a domain, you can do it effortlessly.

Incorporate Best Practices

To have best practices, you actually must *practice* them, not just define them in a "Best Practices Guidelines" document. If there is just one person who doesn't follow them, that person is a weak link in your best practices, and those best practices then are nothing more than a best idea. When I come into companies, I am always curious to know why that company is having issues and why they need me. I go through the first round of meetings to get an idea of the issues and discuss them with the client. Sometimes, from the looks of things, I ask myself,

"What am I going to be able to do here?" The customer and technical folks may seem annoyed that I'm questioning their practices, even though there must be a reason why I am on site. They may insist that they have all the best practices documented, and everyone is supposed to follow them. When I hear this, it's a huge red flag—they may have all of the procedures documented, but it only takes one development manager who hired an employee to get the job done by the business's timeline to throw a wrench in the works—"best practices" are now just a best policy. It is only a "best practice" if it is actually practiced. Let's face it: information will be valuable in the future—you probably have heard that a number of times—but it isn't just the volume of information. You must take actionable steps based on the information provided. Did the information come together in such a way that it helped to make a better decision or to quickly get an answer? The architecture team may assume that the developers are following the best-practices guidelines. Unless the architects do a periodic code review and knowledge transfers to all of the developers; there is no guarantee that they are following your procedures. Keep your best practices limited to the core practices that your applications must follow. Best practices are only as good as the people who follow them. It is much better to have a small set of core practices that people follow than a host of best practices that no one follows. There are best-practices approaches that you can follow when designing systems. The key is in knowing which best practices will produce the best return on investment with the time and resources you have available. You may implement all the best practices in the world but still fail miserably.

Often, I am asked to provide a comprehensive list of best practices that can be used on a daily basis, but many of these best practices are learned over time. I have to wonder if the person asking for the list really understands the complexity of best practices. Also, if I did produce a list and the person's application falls into the exception, what would he do? He probably would tell everyone that my list of best practices was flawed. I think that best practices should be in place but limited to those that will make sense for the company and can be enforced. Think thoroughly through the design, and if you're in doubt about a design or approach, communicate to another peer about the challenge you are working through, or join a chat room or message board. If you are in a position similar to mine, you only know the issues that you have worked through previously. Over time, you may know where to look for issues and solve them faster than someone else, but you can never know the true reason for an issue until you solve it. The challenge is in identifying that it just isn't the coding standards that should be followed;

rather, the whole process needs to adopt best practices, and the best practices should align with a best process.

Perfect the Process

As with any process, you won't simply sit down one day and write the perfect process that works every time for any situation. Processes take time to evolve and over time, your process will become more and more stable. There is a great benefit to having a reliable, repeatable process that gives your people peace of mind and a feeling that when they contribute to the process, they can make a difference. This point is very important to building credibility with the staff, vendors, and others who are working within your process. For the most part, people want to know there is a beginning and end to the work they do. Having an environment that is inconsistent and full of problems really frustrates employees, sometimes to the point that they become apathetic and ineffective. You may find out that no matter how many new employees you hire, the same amount of work gets done. So while it may seem tedious to document, there is a need to have documentation, in some form, to better understand the applications. Simple, concise documents that are easy to maintain and update provide the best chance for success when building your system. The documentation built will be used later as the foundation for the process.

How

The "how" will be explained in the following chapters. I offer the lessons I have learned after working as a consultant for many companies. There is not just one way to solve all challenges; the problems may be similar, but not identical. The solution includes making sure that employees are involved in making the changes. To get their buy-in, you will need to show them there is a better way to run the business. The first step toward change, as a stakeholder in the company, is to admit there is a problem, that you are willing to address it, and that you are committed to fixing the challenges that have occurred over the past months or years. The solution starts in a tactical operation to bring some stability to the systems. Once you have the tactical operations under control, you can move on to the more eloquent solutions, which will prepare your business for success. With a new, sound process in place, you can take on more and more projects with less and less growing pains. Just giving people in the company the satisfaction of working on systems that they know are getting better will make the work environment a lot more palatable. Once you have shown that change is possible and—more importantly—that applications in the company can run more efficiently, the mood in a company starts to change. People who formerly had bad moods will come to work happier and excited to be there. They will start to show ownership of the applications. The good news is that all you need to do to get the entire corporate culture to feel this way is to repeat the process in other departments. Otherwise, if you don't put a process in place to sustain the success you created, the sense of accomplishment may only last a few days or weeks. Once you show employees that there is another way to run business and that progress is possible, there will be a positive shift in the attitude of employees and over time a shift in culture. The *can not* attitude becomes one of *can do*.

FUNDAMENTALS

Fundamental #1: Java

Java is the very core and foundation of the Java application server, as the name implies. It's important to understand Java to some degree, no matter what role you play on the project team. If you are a developer, then you need to command the language. If you are working in a support position or as a project manager working on the project plan, you should understand, at a minimum, the basic construct of Java, where it came from, and what some of its common issues are. If possible, it is best to understand how to read it, write it, read stack traces and most importantly exception handling. You don't need to be a developer to be good at supporting these applications, but it will improve your effectiveness when identifying issues. If you are a developer and are proficient in any programming language, your learning curve will be less than someone who comes from a business background without practical experience in writing code. From a developer perspective, you will need practical understanding of Java; you don't have to be an expert, but having more experience is preferred. When building business applications, you only need to be aware of a few things from a code perspective. For the most part you will use API's in frameworks that are defined by someone else. There may be times when a deep, detailed understanding is important, but for now, it isn't that important.

Systems administrators should be able to read the log files, know what an exception looks like, and be able to follow the applications code. You may not be able to understand everything that is going on, but the more you do understand, the easier it will be to pinpoint issues with code versus configuration. Start looking at log files, and understand when these errors are okay and when they need to be brought to the development team for review. An easy way to get started is to write a Hello World program and deploy it on a Java application server.

As a systems administrator, it will help if you have had the benefit of a Java course or two, but it isn't a requirement. You should at least, however, understand how to set the environments and compile the code. From there you can build a script to automate the build and packaging—and after that, you're in business. From these little successes you can build more success and become more proficient along the way.

Project managers and management should have experiences with Java, too. Their role may be to oversee those areas that the developer needs to look at. Most of the time, it's just a matter of asking simple questions, such as, "Have you checked the log for any error or stack traces?" Your goal as project manager is to keep the mean time to repair at a minimum—or at the very least, be able to ask questions about the components to help narrow down the issues you run into as you build and develop the projects.

Fundamental #2: Application Server

The second fundamental to understand is the application server and how it fits into the *n*-tier paradigm. You won't need to know the details of how the application server is written, but you should be able to set up and configure an application server. Some basic functions of the application server are common across Java application servers. All of the Java application servers will run on a Java Virtual Machine. Internally, the application server will manage (or has the ability to manage) the Java components that you will use within the Java application server for your applications. This includes all the Java components with which you most likely will build your applications; you will write your application logic to use the components of the application server. The benefit is that you can focus on business logic and not worry about managing the technical details of resources, such as Java Database Connectivity (JDBC) or Java Message Service (JMS), for example. You do need to know the differences between the application server configuration files and the annotation in order to turn on these features, for example, transaction management.

You can easily find Hello World applications for each of the various application servers that show how to use each of the components. Once you have experience working with all of the components, you'll get an idea of how you can use these different pieces to build enterprise-level applications. By working with the components, you'll quickly learn the benefits of using each of the application server components.

The developer will need to understand all the various services that need to be configured in order for the application server to work. If you have a JDBC connection or JMS queue setup, he will need to set up one for his testing.

Non-developers should understand how the application server works. They may not have installed or configured one, but I believe that the more they understand about the server, as well as about installation and configuration, the better they will manage time estimates and driving the project plan to completion.

The system administrators need to understand the various tuning capabilities of the system. One of the benefits of having the container manage your application is that you don't have to write as much code. The downside is that the container, out of the box, is not tuned for every environment. You may need to have more memory, threads or other tunable parameters in order to get the best performance.

Fundamental #3: Understand the Operating System

The next fundamental is to understand the operating system on which you are going to deploy your code. There are subtle differences in each operating system (OS)—sometimes even between versions of the same OS—that make a big difference in how your application will perform. It's important to understand the OS and how to use it to your advantage. Your application may be the best-tuned system in the world, but if the application or demand for the resources is constrained by the OS, how will you know if your application is the bottleneck when in fact the bottleneck is due to a configuration system component. Often, having a good understanding of a system and how it works helps in supporting these systems. You may, for instance, run into operating-system issues that look like code issues or network issues. For example, in Windows, one of the most common performance issues in an application has to do with the antivirus software running on the server. The antivirus software can be configured to ignore the applications server libraries, but this is not the default behavior. Without reviewing the antivirus strategy there are serious performance implications for the Java application server, mainly with a hit in performance as much as 50 percent. There are so many components to track that bridging the technological gap and thinking about the system interdependencies takes time and experience.

Other components, such as how the TCP/IP stack in Windows versus UNIX is implemented, may also cause issues with the performance of the application. A lot of the time, I think the perception is that we must hire professionals, and they will know about all these issues. But that is not always the case; I would caution you against relying on one person for all of your information.

Project managers need to understand the operating system impacts as well. They are usually involved with the decisions to purchase the hardware for their application. Have they done their due diligence and investigated some of the issues that may come about with the choice of the operation system? It is their budget that will be in jeopardy when the bill for the hardware comes in, and the system isn't scaling as designed. But how do you know whether you are getting the right hardware and operating system? You may be padding the budget for additional RAM when your system is disk-bound and the additional expense for RAM is unnecessary. Systems administrators are the catchall of these decisions; they are responsible for making the systems work, and most of the time, they are the last ones involved in the process. They have the most need to understand the system and what it takes to keep the system running. Involving systems administrators late in the process may mean that you will have to resolve some of these issues after the applications go to production.

Fundamental #4: Database

One of the first areas I look at when starting to tune a system is the database. The majority of the applications will have a database before they have other downstream systems. Since applications are so heavily dependent on the database, we need to understand, from a granular level, how long each of the database calls take. We should also understand before building a database schema whether we are going to normalize the schema or create a denormalized (a denormalized database is optimizing the design of the database for performance of select and reads) approach to it. There are so many things to understand about the database and design that I could not even begin to cover them, so I will assume that you have a database administrator who has taken all of the above into consideration, and we will consider the database from an application server's perspective.

Developers need to understand how to conservatively access the database—too many calls will cause performance issues. The application server may need to cache some of the database through a lazy initialization to keep that information available, rather than needing to go to the database every time. This will lead to other considerations, such as keeping that cached copy in sync with the database. Another common issue is the use of bind variables in a database. The "bind variable" is a way for the database to know that it has seen this query before and, as a result, it will cache the query you are running but not the dynamic data. A developer would know how to use a prepared statement that takes care of this—it's a best practice, but it's not always followed when companies build applications. Another possibility could be that your developer may, at some time, be responsible for the schema changes and/or creation but doesn't understand what normalization is or when it applies to the database. There can be very serious performance issues that result from this oversight. Non-database administrators and managers should understand that it's just as important that the database administrator have the ability to ask questions and bring in the resources to review the database for performance issues. It also would be beneficial to have some background in structured query language (SQL) and know how to construct queries and or statements. Some important questions that need answers are: How often is the application going back to the database? If it does go back, is there a way to limit the number of times the application goes back to the database? Are we taking advantage of the performance settings in the database that could reduce the number of performance issues? Do we have active participation from the system administrators? (They most likely are going to overcompensate for the database performance issues until the performance issues are resolved because most of the time, they are the front line of defense when things are not going well.)

Fundamental #5: Network

Those who develop support or use the system must have, at the very least, a basic understanding of the network and how the data gets from the Web browser to the application server and back. The network may be one of those areas where you assume everything is working fine and tuned properly; then you find out that the network is the reason for all the performance issues. It's been my experience that as time goes on, we often place trust in the areas that have previously worked, and we stop considering them as a problem. A simple example is the electricity coming to your house—you assume that when you plug your appliance into the wall socket, it will just work. This is the same comfort level I see as people develop these enterprise-level applications. They plug their applications into the wall without thinking about all the settings or the ways in which the network may cause performance issues with the application. Anyone who is technical and works with these systems must understand, at the very least, the basics of a TCP/IP packet and understand the steps that are required to get data from point A to point B. For the most part, you may never need to get down to this level. Your systems will perform well, regardless of the way the network has been configured. But for the 20 percent or more who have applications that are designed in such a way that they require performance-tuned networks, it is necessary to understand the way in which all of these components fit together. When we develop an application, we develop it locally, where we have the advantage of a local request that is much faster than one sent over the Internet. But what if you had to deploy your application into an environment with a 10 megabit half-duplex network instead of a gigabit network?

This is a rare situation, but I have run into it, and it caused numerous performance issues. This issue really tested my ability to reach a detailed level of understanding of how each of the packets is constructed to get the optimal performance for the customer. Most of you will never need to understand, in depth, how a network is working; you can assume it's being taken care of and consider how it works only when you have exhausted all other options in your application. But your job will be a lot easier if you at least understood the number of hops in between nodes and the appliances and/or firewalls that separate these systems. With that relationship, you will understand how issues manifest themselves. At the very minimum, you should know which tool to use to determine if a server is up and running. Some of the most basic and rudimentary commands on your computer may be useful in troubleshooting your issues.

OSI Reference Model

One of the most helpful models—one that I come back to again and again—is the OSI reference model. The OSI reference model defines the multiple layers in the TCP/IP stack and what their function is. That, in itself, isn't too helpful, but the value of this comes when you are building and integrating your *n*-tier applications. Understanding what it takes to get the data packets from one application to another is invaluable in a networked *n*-tier environment. This helps when configuring the load balancer design of coarse grain versus fine grain interfaces, and it also helps with troubleshooting the issues you will encounter in the production arena. The basic construct of the model is that the more you move up the stack from "1" (the wire or physical median, such as copper wire or fiber) toward the seventh layer, the closer you are to the application layer, which is where you have the application code. Understanding this reference model will help you to solve a number of issues and better develop your applications. The challenges will more likely be solved when integrating your load balancers and application. As you move up the stack to the application layer, you reach the application code that builds the presentation for an application.

WHAT IS AN APPLICATION SERVER

There are multiple Java application server providers in the market today. Currently, BEA Systems and IBM hold the top two slots. BEA owns WebLogic; IBM owns WebSphere. WebSphere, JBoss, and Tomcat all have a place in the market, but this book primarily focuses on my WebLogic experience. Given that most of my experience is with WebLogic, some of the techniques I discuss may not be applicable to all application servers. Java application servers are getting more and more feature-rich; it is difficult for me to cover all the key aspects of an applications server. My goal is to give you enough information so that you will understand the basic components. The information provided in this chapter is meant to help you understand some of the main components and, I hope, give you a primer for the rest of this book.

The definition of an application server states that it is first a software engine and second handles its own business logic and data access. The application server by itself does not have any business logic; it requires you to write or purchase and deploy applications on it. This distinction needs to be made, because the application server is the very foundation for all Java applications deployed on them. This is why it is so important to understand the fundamentals, and why the application server is playing such and important role in companies. When you understand the fundamentals, you can work and support any application. The business logic may change, but the core of the server is the same.

Its model—and perhaps a not-so-subtle distinction—is that the Java application server runs on Java. Java is an object-oriented programming language that encourages object reuse. The challenge comes when trying to integrate tens (if not hundreds) of individual components that will constitute your new Web application. You may never see all of these components, but under the cover, the Java application server is built off of other software packages. When we add all of the various components together, it makes for an interesting challenge, which is that it is hard enough to write a software application that can stand on its own;

now you must write an application and support the component applications that it is built and dependent on.

The business application made up of other components is compiled, packaged, and deployed on the Java application server, typically in what is called an EAR (Enterprise Archive, or jar file with a ".ear" file extension) file. The EAR file will contain the custom code that you have written and that will be deployed on the application server. The application that is deployed uses the resources of the application server to connect to enterprise systems. Writing the application for a simple Web application isn't very challenging. Your biggest challenge will be to understand how to design and implement these solutions when you are dealing with multiple integration points. The more experience you have in writing individual components and seeing how they relate, the easier it will be to determine the best architecture strategy for your applications. The tools are defined, but they don't always tell you which one to use at a given time. That is the challenge—that takes working through issues to gain the experience. And it isn't that you just need to get the application to work; you also need to determine how it scales to meet your business needs. Software isn't difficult to understand, but you do need to understand how to write robust code, rather than happy-path code. It is always the exception that gets you, not the expected path.

Managing your own business logic is no small task, either. Do you have the resources available to support the process? Will your choice give you the greatest amount of flexibility? There are choices you'll need to make, and making the wrong choice can waste years of hard work. There are a lot of choices when it comes to managing your business logic, but if you can get it to work together, you will have constructed a useful software application. Using an application server allows you to galvanize your approach to integrating with other systems in your IT organization. And understanding how these systems work allows you to integrate—better and faster—with other businesses.

Applications that are deployed on Java application servers range in complexity from simple, one-page applications to complex enterprise systems that power much of the business systems today. Java application servers provide a consistent way for companies to deploy and manage their applications from the development environment to production. Getting to the application to production is the goal of the application we develop. Using a Java application server provides a common methodology to build systems where all groups must come together to deliver a robust application that meets the increasing demand of the business.

The Java application server allows for us to create applications modularly giving a consistent technical approach to our application design. I think a core benefit is that the Java application server provides a common set of components or services that allows the developer to focus on writing the core business logic. The developer does not have to worry about how to manage resources, such as threads and sockets and memory. Code, which is written by a developer or a code generator that follows these specifications, should be deployable in the containers (application server). To some extent, the Java application server is considered more of a commodity product that enables corporations to build their own business layer on top of it. The real value lies in being able to quickly develop applications that meet the companies' changing business needs. The vendors who are serious about keeping in the application server space are also developing applications on top of the application servers. These applications are making it easier to integrate with the third-party applications, and they provide time to market applications that support complex business needs, not to mention all the third-party logging XML (Extensible Markup Language) parsing tools that are available in Java. Newer technologies and frameworks that are being written for the Java application server appear to be endless and increasing exponentially as time progresses. With the tools and support I would not be surprised to see the Java application server as the dominant technology in all corporations and many small businesses in the near future.

A deficit in the Java application server is that support for these systems can be daunting in many respects. The technology is newer and not everyone has had the experience with them to fully understand how they work. The adoption of the Java application server is high while the detailed understanding of how the server works is still limited. As time goes on there are more and more tools created to support the server management issues.

Containers

A container is a run-time environment that supports a J2EE specification, such as a servlet container or EJB container. You deploy your custom-built code that follows the specification into the container, and there is no need to rewrite your code if you move between vendors. In practice, there may be some changes to the deployment descriptors. A common container is the servlet container in products like Apache/Tomcat. These containers only support servlets and not all of the other specifications defined by the J2EE specification. A full J2EE application server will not only support the servlet container but also all J2EE components, like the EJB container. An example of a J2EE-compliant application server is BEA's WebLogic; it not only supports all the J2EE components, but it also goes through a certification process with Sun Microsystems to be compliant. If you have a simple Web application that does not need to use all the added functionality of clustering and support for enterprise-level components, then you can get away with a simple container that supports only the servlets. If your requirements are that you need support of the other discussed J2EE components, then you most likely will need to have a full J2EE application server.

Getting to Know the Components

With an *n*-tier architecture, there are a lot of components that all must work together to provide the business service. Having a good understanding of the core components is an important step when trying to build applications. You can't expect to become an expert in every area overnight—and you may not want to be—but having the ability to understand how all the parts fit together is an important part of being successful with these business applications. When you understand how all the components are working together, you will be better able to understand the big picture and start providing useful services or applications to the business. It is possible to focus on one area, and some prefer that method, but from my perspective, understanding the system as a whole will give you an advantage over others, and the technology that makes all this happen is Java.

The Java application server adheres to the Java specification. The application server vendors develop their application server accordingly, with some latitude, when it comes to areas not addressed in the specification. Sun Microsystems, which owns the rights to Java, controls the specification. All of the vendors that want to use this specification write their application server according to the Sun specification. The specification defines the following common components: J2EE Connectors, EJB, Java Mail, JDBC, JMS, JMX, JNDI, JSP, JTA, JTS, IDL, RMI/IIOP. The specification defines how the Java application servers implement the various components. By reviewing the specifications, you will understand how the Java application servers interpret the rules. Each vendor then implements its code to adhere to the specification. On top of the vendors' implementation, there are companies that write their business logic and deploy it to the application servers. They package their applications and sell them to you as a bundle. The bundles could be CRM solutions, e-commerce, or a wide variety of other applications. Keep in mind that you won't need a full command of the specification to be successful with application servers, but it doesn't hurt to understand them. I've listed a few that I have worked with over the years. The

complete list of components can be found at the sun Web site: (http://
java.sun.com/j2ee/1.4/docs/).

Every application, to some degree, consists of the common components that
make up the J2EE specifications. The architect chooses the components and
designs your application, using the foundation or building blocks. Sure, the business logic is going to be different, but the components are similar from application to application. This component-based approach is what really distinguishes
the Java application server and the applications you can build on top of it. The
application server provides a software layer that interfaces with databases, messaging, and just about any other software component you can imagine.

Components

Building a reliable, robust business application requires understanding of the
components in the J2EE family. The components should be used conservatively
in the applications only when there is a need to use them. Here's an example: at a
customer site, I was working with an application that used some EJBs (Enterprise
Java Beans). Looking at the JMX monitor, I was able to identify that sixty of the
EJBs they had in the application were configured to be stateful EJBs. A stateful
bean requires that you save state, and it has additional overhead. The customer
was going to production soon and did not have any choice but to use the stateful
session beans in the application. This caused additional hardware to be purchased
to handle all of the additional overhead generated by the overuse of stateful EJBs.
Other examples include users who always enlist transactions inside of the container when there is no requirement to. If you get nothing else out of this Components section, I hope it is clear that you should not overuse the technology just
because it's available. Understand the components and how to tune each resource
for the most effective use of the resources you have.

J2EE Connector Specification 1.5 (J2EE Connectors)

The J2EE Connector specification provides a standard way for enterprise information systems (EIS) to integrate with the Java application servers. The EIS provider will write an adapter that is deployed onto the Java application servers.
Once that resource is deployed, developers can write Java code to communicate
with the EIS system. This is an extremely powerful specification for the enter-

prise, with a way to integrate with existing systems without having to migrate or rewrite the existing legacy system and another reason why Java application servers are so popular—the approach is not to rewrite all your applications in Java; the J2EE Connector gives application servers an API, an application programming interface that allows other applications to access functions to legacy systems. This enables legacy systems to interact with the enterprise in an entirely different way. The ownership is placed on the vendor to provide a way to integrate with its own system, leaving the business a way to leverage their current infrastructure.

J2EE Management Specification (JMX)

The goal of JMX is to provide tools for managing J2EE applications. The management extensions for the servers provide lots of information about the servers, and in my opinion, it is one of the most valuable tools for managing an application. There are a number of tools and vendors on the market that you can use to connect to your Java application server and get all sorts of information about the servers and their health state. The enterprise uses the JMX monitors for production-monitoring load testing and getting more information about the servers. While you can use tools to connect to the servers and get information, you can also write you own programs to monitor your systems. I have used the JMX extensively to identify patterns and gain metrics on the application servers with which I have worked.

Enterprise JavaBeans Specification (EJB)

EJBs enable Java developers to create distributable, portal code that can be configured to enlist transactions and runs inside of the Java application server. The purpose of the EJB code is to support the business logic of the application without worrying about the details of how the container manages the resources, such as threads memory and transactions. There is a lot of benefit to using used EJBs in enterprise applications that require scalable solutions. There is additional management and configuration when building and writing EJBs, and you need to be careful when using them. If there is one downside to the EJB, it's that in some cases it is overprescribed when developing J2EE applications. There are three basic types of EJBs: session beans, entity beans, and message-driven beans. Session beans are additionally divided into stateful session beans and stateless session beans. Like all of the components, there is a time and place to use an entity bean or a stateful session bean; overuse of the component can lead to performance issues.

Java IDL API

The Java IDL is a way for the Java application server to invoke operations on a remote resource, using IDL rather than RMI. The basic difference is that Java IDL is for CORBA developers who want to write code in Java, but who also want to write to the CORBA IDL interface. The fundamental difference lies in whether you want to do a remote-method invocation using Java IDL or RMI-IIOP. Unless you have a client with CORBA, you will not need to use this, but given that I have run into issues with it, I thought it worthwhile to mention.

Java Naming and Directory Interface (JNDI) Specification 1.2.1

JNDI is a directory for application servers to publish and look up services. Services publish the location for their services in the JNDI tree, and when you (as a developer) need to use a particular resource, you look up that resource in the tree. The main issue you may run into with JNDI is in being able to find the resource for which you are looking. In a cluster, you may not be able to find a resource because of an issue that replicates the resource. The way to look at the JNDI is as a lookup table for Java resources that are deployed to the application server. It's absolutely critical to understand how to look up resources in an application server.

Java Message Service (JMS) Specification

JMS provides a reliable, asynchronous way for the enterprise to exchange business data throughout the enterprise. This is an extremely powerful component that allows you to send or receive messages with applications in enterprise. The messages can also be configured to be persistent; in the event of a server crash you won't lose your data. With all components, there are configuration settings that are just as important as the written code. Most of the issues I run into with JMS are configuration-related due to lack of time or resources to properly configure the resources for the business needs. Used correctly in the enterprise, JMS provides a critical component for exchanging of enterprise data in the enterprise. I think one of the most valuable uses of JMS is to decouple composite applications, which, if configured correctly, will eliminate dependencies for your downstream applications.

Java Servlet Specification (Servlets)

Servlets are the key behind making a Web application possible, and they provide the control for the MVC (Model-View-Controller) architecture. While you can custom-write your own servlets, popular direction is leaning more toward using a framework that handles the complexities for you. Using a framework, you will most likely indirectly work with servlets, rather than writing servlet code directly. These are key concepts that you will find helpful when troubleshooting issues and understanding how the servlet works. Understanding how the framework uses servlets will help you with the issues you run into.

Java Transaction API (JTA) Specification

Managing transactions in a Java application server is very important with business transactions. For example, you would not want a bank to debit your account before crediting another account (or perhaps you *would* want that to happen but only if it was in your favor). There are multiple ways to enlist some business logic in a transaction. You can start the transaction yourself or let the container do it for you. As with any component, knowing when to use a resource is sometimes more important than not using the resource at all.

JDBC Specifications

A common integration point for the application server is the database. The benefit of the database is that it allows you to persist and store data for your application. To access the database, you need to have an interface to which you can write code and to which you can talk; that, in turn, will talk directly to the database. The application server may be bundled with some JDBC drivers, or you might use the database vendor's drivers. You will need to be cognizant of the version of driver you are using, and make sure that the application server supports it. Creating your custom components in J2EE gives you the ability to automatically create database tables and data-related components. Keep in mind that the same database rules apply on these dynamically generated components as apply to the basic database performance-tuning ideas.

Java Server Pages (JSP) Specification

Written as an extension to servlets, the JSP allows the developer to write the user interface for the application. The JSP is much more like HTML than writing a servlet and is commonly used for the view (V) in the MVC architecture. One of the biggest issues with JSPs is to keep developers from putting their business logic inside of the JSP. It may seem easier at first to do this, but it may lead to issues down the road when trying to scale the application to meet the business needs.

RMI/IIOP

RMI/IIOP allows Java developers to write in Java-remote interfaces to build truly distributed applications. The developers can write the application code as if they were local, and through configuration, it can communicate with remote servers as if they are local. Using RMI can be innocuous by itself; the issues arise when you deploy your applications in separate clusters. When you build an application, decouple the business logic from the presentation, and deploy it on separate hardware, you need to be sure that you are using a fairly coarse-grained call. If you make a number of fine-grained calls to a server, you can end up adding latency to the application call, as well as adding a real performance hit. One of the biggest issues I see when customers implement their applications is that they may not be aware of how the application will be deployed in production. Keep in mind that remote calls add overhead and may be a performance killer to your application.

Components that Drive the SOA Initiative

As revolutionary as the Java application server itself is, the concept of service-oriented architecture and the value it can bring to the enterprise is even more revolutionary. The service-oriented concept is not new by any respect, but until recently, the enterprise did not have the ability to adopt the architecture without the advance in chip speeds, improved memory management of virtual machines, maturation of the Java application server, and the components built to support it. As with any architectural pattern, the service-oriented pattern is built on all of the concepts and components that are discussed in this book—the application to the SOA architectures and the foundation for the applications that give you the ability to implement SOA architecture. Some of these specifications give you the opportunity to build a service-oriented architecture of the future.

Java API for XML Registries Specification 1.0

The specification provides the API definition on how to access different kinds of XML registries. The XML registries are infrastructure for building and deploying Web services. The definition allows us to provide a master way to access Web services throughout the enterprise. Discovering and finding Web services allows us to route traffic for specific Web services though configuration rather than using code. With the ability to route based on code you can eliminate the dependencies between applications and give flexibility to support versioning of applications and ease of administration.

Java API's for XML/SOAP

SOAP with Attachments API for Java Specification
Java API for XML Processing Specification
Java API for XML-based RPC Specification

Using the common XML/SOAP API's to transmit data from one interface allows us to open up our application interfaces to applications other than Java. The interface signatures on Java application servers can be called by a non-Java application by adhering to the specifications. This is what really allows us to start transformation of the business enterprise from a tightly coupled interface to a loosely coupled interface that can interact across multiple technologies. These specifications are some of the main reasons that composite applications, written in different programming languages, can talk to each other through a defined interface. SOAP provides a lot of advantages to these interfaces but at a cost of performance and may require additional resources. Extensive use of SOAP has been discouraged in the enterprise application, primarily for the performance issues.

DESIGNING AN APPLICATION FOR SUCCESS

Why Design Systems

We design systems so that our implementation of the system matches our vision. We want the system to meet some business need, and when you are on a key project that can accomplish the implementation, there is no better feeling than executing a project that is helping to grow the business. Management will notice the work you're doing—you'll get a prime parking spot or whatever other perk the company warrants to show its appreciation for the work you've done. Conversely, there is no worse feeling than spending a year on a project, only to see the project fail. It is frustrating to come in every day to another problem that you helped design or to realize that it's your fault that the systems are not up and running.

Multiple independent components are what make up the application as a whole, from user interfaces all the way down to the database. When we buy a packaged application, we also get the benefits of the design process. When we purchase a package, we purchase the implementation of that application. We design the data for the system, where the data is going to reside, how we access it, and which business logic we need to make this work. Time is spent on the application design to determine how the application will pass data back and forth between the business layers. Many companies also spend time designing the overall process for how these systems and applications will work together. So we spend time designing the application architecture and system, but we fail to design our performance-stability plans. We fail to design the transition plans for employees. We fail to get past the physical components of the application to realize there is more than just the components in the application that need to work together.

Plan for Failure

If you were to stand up in a meeting and say, "You know, I think we should plan for failure," you might get some strange looks. Who wants to plan for failure? That's not the way to design a system. It's common knowledge that the Happy Path code is always the easiest to write. Take any simple Hello Word application built, and compile it locally. Works great, but when you try to change the code or do anything other than what the example shows, it will break. The comment from the developer is always, "I can get the code working on my desktop." And this pattern of the code not working isn't only to the first environment; it also happens as you move the code from environment to environment. The developer will research the issue and find the execution path is different than what he expected in the environment.

What separates a good developer from a bad one is that the good developer is able to predict the failure paths and account for them *before* writing and deploying the code. When designing systems that you know are going to interact with remote services, plan for failure. Have a plan so that when the application is in production, the dependent system is not available. How will the system react? How can you gracefully handle the exceptions and show the customer something useful, rather than just an exception page? Do you want to take the burden off the customer by handling it for him, so that he doesn't need to retry his submission? I think everyone is guilty, at times, of just doing the basics to "get by" at work. But if you can adopt the habit of always planning for the exceptions, you will help to manage the process, rather than letting the process manage you. Invariably, you are going to have to fix that issue sooner or later. Why not plan for it ahead of time? Such planning helps you to manage the customer's expectations, which leads to customer satisfaction.

Reach Out

There is nothing more frustrating than having a job to do and not being able to do it. Or you have enough time to do it, but you just haven't had the experience. Or you know of one way to do it that has worked in other situations, but you're not sure if it will work now. Reach out to other engineers and external resources for clarification and support on an issue when you may not be 100 percent clear on it. It is a win-win situation for you and your coworkers. Your solution may be the right solution, but it's still good to involve others in the decision-making process. By adopting this strategy, you'll gain knowledge much faster than by sitting alone in front of a computer, pulling out your hair in frustration. When you exchange ideas and build technical relationships, you galvanize toward a common goal. This will greatly reduce the number of issues and will help you to develop better systems—systems that cause you less trouble at night and give you the satisfaction of a job well done after working on a successful project.

Physical Design

A typical design session takes place to negotiate the application design and to determine how the application will meet the business goals. This is most important early on in the design of the application, when the goal is to take the business requirements and figure out how to make the application a reality. The deficit in the design meetings is the way in which we design for the production environments. Some people may say, "Well, we are planning for production." I guarantee that even if you have planned for production, there will be issues and things you did not think of. Think of all the ways you failed in the past—now, how can you apply that to the current design? There needs to be an understanding of how the systems application design may affect the success of the application. Take the lessons learned from your environments and apply those to these designs. How will the physical design of the system work with the application design? I will give you a "for instance":

When a large telecommunications company designed systems, they always made designs with the assumption that distance was not a factor—if a database was in Texas, and the application was in Los Angeles, that was okay. The application architects, however, built their systems to work on an application that had the database and application deployed locally. The challenge this presents is that the development and testing efforts were all done on systems that anticipated the application would be local. What are some of the problems this company faced? They faced many; for example, any time a backhoe dug up a fiber line between Los Angeles and Texas, the whole enterprise would practically shut down. They would run into bandwidth issues when traffic increased; the connection between the two data centers would get overloaded. In my experience, most companies don't think about the physical location of their servers when designing systems. Although I may see this as a common situation, I am usually brought in to the companies that are having difficulties. I do hear, however, a lot about the problems caused by systems that are physically separated. This is a design that should be taken into account during the design process.

Production Hardware

If possible, always use the same hardware that you will use when going to production. If you try to get by on less, you will probably suffer the consequences later, when trying to get these systems working in production. Complex systems can have an unlimited number of issues. If you are working with an operating system that is familiar to you, your odds of success are much greater. I have found that a large number of issues do arise when moving to production on hardware that's different from that used to develop the application. The hardware on which you deploy has just as much impact as the code. It becomes an extremely costly mistake if you pick the wrong version of the operation system or hardware. Many decisions must be made before choosing one operation system vendor over another. There are no vendors who haven't, at some point, released a buggy operation system or hardware vendor who have never had hardware issues.

The choices you have for an operating system are fairly limited to Windows- and UNIX-based systems. There are multiple versions from which to choose, but for the most part, these are your two choices. Choosing a Windows-based operating system over a UNIX system has both advantages and disadvantages. Based on my experience, I find the UNIX systems are easier to manage. That may be because I feel more comfortable in a UNIX environment. I know how to configure the systems and optimize them to meet my needs. UNIX may not be the right choice for everyone, if you don't have the economies of scale or you need to retool your entire IT department to start supporting UNIX systems. Then you may have a complete and utter failure if you choose to go this route. Choosing an operating system is like hiring an employee—he may have all the right qualifications and a great résumé, but if he doesn't fit the organizational culture, his chance of success is limited.

Keep in mind that you can fail when trying to switch technologies if you bring in a new technology that alienates your employees, even though you know that the direction in which you are going will help the business in the long term. It is important to involve the stakeholders in the company. If you plan on undergoing the transition, consider those who are going to support and maintain these systems. Having their support is important to the success of the project. Understand that there is a tremendous learning curve, and support them during the transformation process. Choosing the right operating system and hardware will impact how easy this system is to support. UNIX operating systems lend themselves easily to scripting and automation; Windows operating systems have more tools built for them. Windows operating systems may prove more prone to virus attacks; UNIX operating systems mostly need to be concerned with worms. In any event, you should plan your operating system based on the security requirements for your environment.

Service Level Agreements

When it comes to service level agreements, not having one—or having an extremely generic one—is most often the case. I've often asked about the goals of an application and have been given a generic response. For example, someone might tell me that every transaction should be four seconds or less, or they say they haven't had a chance to look at the application yet, but if everything came back in a second, that would be good. Most of the time, these numbers are a best guess, picked up from talking with business analysts. To truly understand the service level agreements, you really must prove them out over time and update as you get farther into production. To meet the service level agreements, you must include them in the upfront design of the system. If you say a system must respond in four seconds, and you have servers distributed all across the globe that are dependent on those responses, then how practical is this request?

Web Metrics Are Inaccurate

Application metrics can be misleading when working with an application—and especially misleading when working with a large cluster. Companies that measure the performance of their applications by sending a synthetic transaction through the application have a false sense of security. To know the true availability of a system, you would need to know about every customer experience. Who had issues and who didn't? The challenge with services that send these synthetic transactions through your Web site is the frequency of data that is measured and the number of requests. The applications get data—say, every fifteen minutes or so—and over an hour, you have four log-ins. But consider that you have twenty thousand unique log-ins in an hour. The 4/20,000 log-ins is statistically insignificant. With twenty thousand log-ins, you will have millions of transactions, and even though the synthetic transaction shows success, you may still be getting exceptions. Customers will complain, even when you have successful metrics on your monitoring tools. Web metrics are great from a macro level, but you should not be basing your bonuses on such a small sample, because while the customer experience may be horrible, your numbers look really good.

The business owner brings up the issue of performance to the engineering group and says he has been getting a lot of complaints from the end users about availability. Blank screens. Unexpected behavior. We all have had this happen at one point or another. There are two scenarios that a developer or engineers can take regarding the quality issue with the site. The poor engineer will cite the metrics and say that everything looks okay because the numbers look good. The good engineer will dig down into the issues and determine that the numbers are wrong. When you have a sampling that is as small as the one above, you cannot believe it—in this case, it tends to be inaccurate. You may assume that I personally don't support Web metrics, but this isn't the case. These tools are great for giving an overall view, on a macro level, of how the servers are doing. I think you need to have this data, and take it to heart when working through issues. The key with this data, though, as with any piece of information, is that it is only one data point.

Build Process In

To test the process we must have results; the more results we have, the better we will be able to measure success and determine if the process is working. The best way to get those results is to repeat the process, or, iterate through the process. With an iterative process, you take the information learned from the previous iteration and plug that into the current one. This strategy of continual improvement will harden the environments and build more repeatable results. Having an engineer solve problems is part of the daily activities in a software organization. The more you solve the problems, the more you become adept at solving them. What's often missing is the process that takes lessons learned from other environments and communicates back to the development environments. The challenge for the engineer is to get consistent input, as well as being rewarded when he follows the process. Determining the difference in a high-performing information-technology shop from a poor-performing one is relatively easy—you will know within a few minutes of interviewing key people. The poor-performing shops are filled with poor process. A few people own all of the knowledge about the system. There will always be mistakes building and deploying any system; the question is, "Are we making the same mistake once or multiple times?" If the answer is the same mistakes multiple times we are not learning from the mistakes by accounting for them in our process.

Evolve or Die

We are faced with difficult challenges every day, in the workplace, at home, and just life in general. I know that I must make decisions every day that force me to evolve in some way. Whether it is due to competition or to keep current, if I don't keep up with technology my technical abilities will stagnate and ultimately my value to the market will diminish to a point where my skill set is no longer needed. Applications face new challenges every day. They are forced to either change to compete and evolve, or they will, over time, provide diminishing returns. For example, let's say that your business has doubled since last year—such a challenge is a hope you had when you put a new program in place. The challenge, however, should not be that you grew and now cannot handle your business. Instead, the challenge should be how you will evolve your process and business to accept the challenge. Being able to accept the challenge is a lot of what this book is about—how systems evolve when challenged with environmental challenges.

Application Traits

How can you determine if an application is successful? For starters, people are using the systems. In using the system, you are either saving the company money or making money for the company. The successful applications on which I have worked have a few key traits. These applications may not have been the best-performing applications to begin with, but over time, they became stellar performers. They became those performers by resolving issues, documenting the process, implementing new process, and transitioning knowledge to others. If you can master these simple process steps, your chance for success will increase. The process of resolving, documenting, implementing, and transitioning is done hundreds of times on an application. This is not one big effort; rather, it should be accomplished daily, perhaps even hourly in the beginning, to get the application up to a level where you can see a return on your investment.

Resolve: You need to be able to resolve the technical challenges that are facing you. How you resolve them is up to you and your company's technical prowess. When you have all the technical muscle you need, then resolving issues is easy.

Document: Document your findings. Typically, these issues will manifest themselves in another environment or another form. When you don't have a record of this, you are less likely to remember it. Then, the only people who are aware of these issues are those who are directly involved.

Implement: Having the resolution and implementing it are two different things. How do you take the lessons learned and implement them into your systems?

Transition: Being able to transition knowledge to other team members or groups is very important. The transition may be in the form of release notes or a knowledge base. A good repository with critical information should be available.

Developing Quality Applications

Java Standards

As important as the Java code itself is, you must also have a defined set of standards that all developers use to make the application as consistent as possible. There is always more than one way to solve a problem with code—if you solve the problem ten different ways in ten different applications, you will create an application that is difficult to support and hard to follow. This is the beginning of a spaghetti code that leads to tribal knowledge and just creates a lose-lose situation for all involved. The biggest challenges I have seen with application code, as well as some of the most painful issues, have been with developers who tried to get the container (application server) to do something it clearly wasn't designed to do. By choosing this path, you will exercise code that, for all intents and purposes, isn't used by the majority of application servers. And you will run into an issue sooner or later. My best example of this is a developer who found a way to his own threads inside of an EJB. This caused problems—big problems—so much so that the application was down for hours at a time during the day. The reason he had to do this was that the data he needed came from an enterprise system, and the system did not have a coarse-grained call to return all the data he needed. So he decided that he would thread the call, get back the data in parallel, and increase performance. While this is an approach, it caused more problems than it fixed. The right approach is to push that requirement back on the enterprise system in a single request, rather than making five smaller ones.

Standards

Having good standards in place is easy to do when there is an agreement on the approach, and you have ample time to implement and plenty of time to work with the business on the requirements. While this technique may work well if you are designing a spaceship or rocket, where you have the time to build the system right, with the business application there is no luxury of time. If we wait for all the requirements before building the application, the business opportunity might be gone, or we would lose so much market share that we could not compete. We know that we have to have standards, but how can we create standards in an environment that is changing so rapidly? This is never an easy assignment; it must be done on a small scale and replicated out to smaller projects. On a large scale, the organizational culture has to change to support these changes. On a small scale, this can be accomplished by a team that works together. Think about a game of tug-of-war: The objective is to have two teams opposing each other with one rope. To be successful with the game, your team has to pull harder than the other team. If I asked you for your strategy for wining the game, you most likely would say, "Let's get the strongest people and have them on our team. We'll get someone to be the anchor at the end of the rope and improve our chances for success."

When it comes time to build applications, the same philosophy should be used. First and foremost, define the objective. The objective in tug-of-war is simple: pull the other team across the line. The objective in building application is no different: build a high-performing application. We do that by getting the strongest person as the anchor and then having the team members pull in the same direction. It doesn't really matter which technology you use, as long as your team members are all working together toward the common goal. When you define standards, keep them simple. Make the goal something that all can achieve. There is only one direction; everyone should pull in that direction.

Copy and Paste

When you are looking for issues in your application code, don't rule out issues related to cutting and pasting of code. In development, the reality is that cutting and pasting is common practice, where the code is cut from the Web or other samples. This is a great way to get your code up and running quickly, but use caution when doing so. I once ran into an issue where someone solved a problem with a sample code. This was a portal application, so other developers needed to implement a portlet inside of a portal application. The developer unknowingly copied and pasted a memory leak into several other places in the application. This developer then took the code and shared it with a third developer. All told, the code was copied three times into various places in the application. The application servers had been crashing and running into "OutOfMemory" errors. Although we found the issue with the memory leak, we didn't think to look other places. We pushed the code, and the servers all crashed after three days instead of two; this process continued one more time. The point is that even though you fix a code issue in the code itself, always check for common occurrences in the rest of the code.

It is okay to copy and paste code; we have all done it to get an application built in a timely manner. The key is to go back to review the code you have copied. You may find a sample online that meets your objective, but what are the pros and cons of using this approach? Even from a simple perspective, is it the right approach for performance? Is it in line with your development standards? Even more importantly, do you understand what the code is doing?

Code Review

No matter how strapped you are for time, you must do code reviews. The code review basically is a way for a senior developer or peer to review what the code developers write. In business applications, some teams do code reviews, but that is not usually the norm. I think the code review is important for the health of the application and for keeping your peer developers aware of what you are doing. In addition to keeping other developers apprised of your activities and what the code does, you can also check to make sure they are not violating corporate policy. Are developers capturing data from systems and passing it on to an e-mail address or direct-file writes? You may also find that both development groups are writing code to solve the same business problem. You could be working together to solve the same problem, rather than working in parallel on a similar effort.

Dependent Systems

When writing your code, and especially when you are interfacing with another system, always code for the worst case. That is, if you have an application that requires an http request, what are the likely scenarios that you should be able to handle? A common one is if you can't get the resources but need to consider all the exception paths. What happens if the server is down for an hour or a day without that resource? A good developer doesn't just write the code to meet the needs of the current application; a good developer has the ability to predict an issue he might run into, and he can mitigate it before it happens.

SOME COMMON ARCHITECTURAL PATTERNS

When I discuss design patterns, people's eyes glaze over. I feel like I have lost them before the conversation even starts. Essentially, a design pattern is a solution that has been successfully used to solve a problem. We take that pattern and apply it to an issue when the problems appear to be similar in nature. For example, when building a house, you have certain design patterns that are in place to solve issues. Let's say you are putting a fireplace in the house. It sounds simple enough. Many houses have fireplaces, but let's suppose you decide not to follow the design pattern of putting a chimney on that fireplace. Now you have a fireplace in a house without a chimney. What is going to happen when you light a fire for the first time? You will have smoke in the house. This is fundamentally the same idea when building applications. The design patterns are very similar to putting a chimney on a fireplace.

I am going to discuss some of the main architectural patterns. (If you want more detail than is described here, patterns are prevalent on the Internet.) The most important pattern you should be well versed in the MVC (Model-view-controller).

Some Architectural Patterns

Model-view-controller
Presentation-abstraction-control
Client-server
Three-tier
Service-oriented architecture
Pipeline
Implicit invocation
Observer pattern

Blackboard system
Peer-to-peer
Broker Pattern

MVC Architecture

One of the most common patterns used is the Model-View-Controller (MVC). MVC is the most popular for design patterns for business applications deployed on Java application servers. The basic construct is to decouple the main layers of the application to reduce the amount of changes you need to make to the layers when making code changes. So if you need to add additional business logic to an application, you can easily add a new business component and a new Java server page (JSP) without having to make big changes to all JSPs.

Model: The model represents the enterprise data and the business rules that govern access to and updates of this data. The model often serves as a software approximation to a real-world process, so simple real-world modeling techniques apply when defining the model.

View: JSPs and HTML commonly comprise the view or presentation layer. The presentation layer displays the contents to the end user.

Controller: The controller is the servlets that hold logic to communicate with the EJBs in the model layer.

The controller handles the interactions with the view (represented by a Java servlet), and data requests to be performed by the model. The controller acts as a delegate and delegates work to other components. The controller determines which requests will be sent to get data from business processes and controls the state of the data perhaps through session or a form. Based on the user request the data from the model will vary. The controller responds by selecting an appropriate view. The view renders the contents of a model through which it accesses enterprise data, the model, and determines how that data should be presented. It is the controllers' responsibility to show the appropriate views based on the applications design. You can either write your own controllers or use one of the many frameworks available. "Struts" is a great example of a framework that people use to create applications. Struts is the controller in MVC; you would need to have a good data-access layer to be MVC. People are coming up with more ways to build and develop tools that allow you to automate building of Java applications.

It is a really good idea to start by building and deploying sample applications using these technologies. The more you use them, the better understanding you'll have and better the marketability of your skills. When you understand the basic concepts and constructs of the applications, you will realize that these concepts aren't complex—it just feels that way when they all come at you at once.

Client-Server

As the name suggests the client-server model probably is one of the ones with which you are most familiar. This model is found everywhere, like non-Web-based e-mail, printers, and many other applications. The way I look at it, there is a client that stands independent of the server application. If the server goes down, you will still have your client running; the client doesn't go down, only the server. Your Web browser is a client that interacts with your Java application server. You will run into this pattern less often with the MVC, but it is common with Java applications.

N-Tier

A common architectural pattern is the *n*-tier architecture. The main advantage to using *n*-tier architecture is that each of the components can be reused and upgraded independently. The technical difference between the MVC architectural pattern and the *n*-tier pattern is that with the *n*-tier pattern, the component can be upgraded independently. In the MVC architecture all components may be interdependent. The Java application server is commonly used in the *n*-tier architecture. The Web server handles the static content; application does the dynamic content, and the database that has the data. Most of this book deals with the issues that come up in an *n*-tier architecture.

Service-Oriented Architecture

The service-oriented architecture (SOA) has received a lot of buzz within the enterprise as of late. SOA can be Java or other technologies. Adopting an SOA approach to software design is a loose coupling of your business software interfaces. This is an incredible benefit to the IT world. A lot of the availability issues in working with the composite applications could be resolved by going to SOA architecture. The current non-SOA architectures require incredibly tight coupling between the applications—an issue you will see when you read further in the book.

As an architect for a Fortune 100 company, I witnessed firsthand the downside of a non-SOA architecture. The architecture was so tightly coupled that if one component in the business layer went down, six hundred production pagers all went off, and six hundred employees had to spend an hour or so of their time responding to these pagers. That is not to say that we could have solved the entire problem with SOA, but if the company thought of its components as services to clients, I think the availability of the applications would have been better.

The second challenge I saw for which SOA might have saved time and money was with the deployment strategy of the IT department. Each time there was a change in the business layers, all 256 applications had to prepare for the changes and code those changes. Once a year or more, the whole IT department had to coordinate hundreds of implementation plans to simultaneously push code to meet the business level changes. Not only was it a tremendous amount of work to push all the code, but imagine the amount of troubleshooting involved when trying to test all these applications. SOA is building a lot of momentum, especially when it's implemented in a modular fashion in key strategic areas. When making the shift to SOA architecture, my advice is to plan your strategy carefully. Start with a key application, deploy, develop, and understand what the most successful process is to support this system.

Common Design Patterns

If you are supporting or administering a J2EE site, you will probably have heard about design patterns. Design patterns are a very fine-grained-detail type of development, but the chart below shows some of the more common patterns.

The chart below has some of the common patterns.

Common Development Patterns	Common J2EE Design Patterns
Abstract Factory	Business Delegate
Bridge	Composite Entity
Builder	Composite View
Chain of Responsibility	Data Access Object
Decorator	Dispatcher View
Iterator	Intercepting Filter
Factory Method	Session Facade
Flyweight	Service Locator Pattern
Model View Controller II	Value List Handler
Memento	Value Object
Mediator	Value Object Assembler
State	View Helper
Strategy	Service to Worker
Prototype	Service Locator
Singleton	

Why Patterns

Understanding the theory behind the patterns is important, but understanding the patterns and being able to troubleshoot the issues in production takes a very different thought process. A design pattern is essentially a solution to a design problem that can be used to solve the same problem in different situations. To be successful with the Java application server, you should understand the basic design patterns. You will run across most of the design patterns from time to time but others you'll see rarely, if ever. There is no "right" pattern to use for all situations. When troubleshooting a performance issue, start looking at the design after you have ruled out the environmental issue. You have done all you can with the application and at some point you must focus on the application and how it was implemented. There is no alternative except to evaluate the architecture and how the application was designed.

MVC in Practice

If you are using an application server, then you are probably using the MVC architectural pattern. And if you separate out the static content and use a database, you also have an *n*-tier architecture. The MVC pattern separates your database code from your application code. The theory is that you now have a defined interface between the business and database. Work done in the business layer can be changed without having to rework your presentation code. This may seem oversimplified, but that is the basic construct. When you have a large application, it is difficult to keep all the developers following this pattern, especially if you have new developers. Invariably, some will violate the rule from time to time. When looking at applications, check to make sure that developers have not done this. An example of this would be in the presentation layer, or JSP. Let's say that a developer has decided that he needs to get data from the database and present that data. The developer either creates his own connection or goes through the JCBC connection pools to get the data needed and display it. Going to the database directly is a violation of the rule, but it is very common to find this in older applications. From an administration perspective, this causes many problems. The administrator monitors the connection pools but will not see the database connection being used. Additional complexity has been added to the application that makes it hard to trace. If there is another JSP that needs access to the database, it will most likely copy the code. Now you have two places to look when trying to debug the code. Using the Java application server components gives you a common way for developers to write code with less chance of violating the best practices. There are still going to be occasions when they violate the policy, but having a common way to do things in place, with code reviews, will keep those incidents down.

Service Locator

The service locator is another common design pattern. The service locator is a simple interface in which you can look up all the services you are going to use. When you need to get access to a service in the application, you use the service locator, rather than writing the code in multiple places to get the service. The most common implementation of this is when it is time to get the initial context. Enterprise applications need to look up service objects. When they look them up, it is expensive; it is a performance hit. This is one of the patterns that I find in application very frequently. A simple example is that there are two departments writing two different applications. They may have a requirement to look up a service. Simple implementation gets the connection to the remote resource and does the lookup, gets back some data, and you are done. The problem is that this was done on a one-off lookup. When the business requires an additional lookup, the code is copied and pasted, rather than looked up. The pattern continues until you have multiple places to check and update when trying to troubleshoot your code. Encourage the code reuse and have a single place for developers to look when making modifications to the code. Now, if your application only needs to look up the context once, then perhaps you don't need the service locator pattern. Using the pattern is related to how much work it will save you to use it versus the amount of time to write it. Sometimes, it is simply common sense whether or not to use the patterns.

Singleton

A common pattern that I see over and over again is the singleton. The singleton pattern ensures that there is only one instance of the class per instance of class loader. The singleton is helpful when you want to have only one instance of an object in application servers, such as a data cache or the service locator. The issue you will encounter in a large cluster is that you will have one singleton per managed application server. Assuming you have a cluster of three, you would have this instance repeated three times.

Here's an example: in the application layer of a billing application, the customer was using a service locator design pattern with a singleton to cache the references to the remote servers. The customer described several issues that, to me, seemed like very odd behavior. The "thread dumps" from the servers showed all threads blocking on the one class. The singleton did a lookup on a resource every ten minutes. When the resource was down, the singleton was stuck in a synchronized method and was blocked. The whole application would go down from time to time because of this. This is why you need to make sure that your singleton is thread-safe; the singleton needed to update every so often based on a timer. I inquired as to why they handled the routing through their own singleton class—the more complex you make the helper classes, the more issues you are going to encounter. Let the Java application servers handle the clustering and failover. Also, keep in mind that if you are forced into using this type of pattern, realize what happens when the dependent applications are down. In this case, the customer did not test all scenarios and, as a result, ran into problems in production.

Another interesting issue I ran into with the singleton was when we deployed and undeployed the applications. There was some logging that the customer had put into the code to track an issue. After redeploying the software application, we noticed that the log file was still being updated. This indicated that the singleton was still alive and doing work. The problem here was that the singleton class was located in a jar file in the system class path. After an auto-deploy, or redeploy, the singleton class never got initialized because of its location in the system-level class path.

Another issue we encountered was that the first request seemed to work but subsequent requests did not, and it seemed to be fairly random. This manifested itself mostly during high-load scenarios. The controller was making a remote call to another EJB cluster that was running a packaged application. The EJB application cluster had five unique clusters, and each connected to a set of Tuxedo servers. The cached context of the remote EJB servers had been given a cluster address of the virtual IP, so the IP address of the cluster was a virtual IP that mapped to five separate WebLogic EJB clusters. WebLogic (the application server being used) negotiated each initial context. Because the EJB server's cluster address was used by the EJB handle to build the connection string, the first requests worked but state was quickly lost. Not surprisingly, the error only occurred when two or more clusters had been running, because the VIP contained references to multiple clusters that were homogenous but were distributed among five separate clusters that were not able to failover properly. To make it more complex, the first request went through the load balancer and then went directly through the server. Communication through the virtual IP was not guaranteed. The point I am trying to make is that the application architecture can dictate the complexity; the more complex the architecture the more workarounds you may need to have.

Frameworks

Time to market is extremely important for most business applications. As a result, frameworks have come about to provide a way for rapid deployment and development of applications that conform to design specifications. This is accomplished by using integrated development environments (IDEs) and tools to quickly build the enterprise JavaBeans (EJBs) and other Java components. Using a framework, you can, to some degree, rely on the framework to follow the specification and provide you with a compliant application, if you choose to use its software. The trend, which isn't changing, is to use frameworks as the base for your application. The biggest benefit to using a framework is in the process that comes with the framework. (If you adopt the framework, you also must adopt the process that is built into the application.)

The second benefit of using the framework is that there are engineers who specialize in one or more frameworks. When you need to build your application, you don't need to just look for a Java developer. Instead, you can narrow your focus to a Java developer with experience in that focused area. The use of frameworks to build out Java applications is increasing, and I don't see this changing in the near future. They are just too powerful and give us the ability to quickly build complex applications with relative ease.

Struts

Struts is an open-source framework that provides the "controller" of the model-view-controller architectural pattern. The Struts framework allows you to integrate with third-party packages and data access technologies. The combination of struts, together with the other components, provides an MVC architectural framework that you can use to build your applications. Struts is one of the frameworks on which a number of other companies are building their frameworks, and it can be found in commercially available software as well. There is a lot to understanding all the ins and outs of Struts, but I think it is key to have some exposure to the framework and understand how that technology is used in applications. If I were to choose only one framework with which you should start working, it would be Struts. One downside, however, to using a framework—or any third-party jar, for that matter—is that you are increasing the chances of adding a bug that is beyond your control. It may require a custom patch or waiting for the next release to fix your bug. In addition to the bug, if you upgrade your application server, you will need to make sure the new jars are supported in the application server. For example, let's say you are using Struts 1.1, and you need to integrate with a menu component that is Struts 1.2.9—this may cause you to run into an issue.

APPLICATION MANAGEMENT

Stabilize the Environment

Once you have the code written and deployed, the next biggest challenge is the environment. This process can be difficult, if not almost impossible, without a repeatable process or plan to follow. With your application code, a big consideration is with moving it from one environment to another. However it may only involve environmental changes. These environment issues range from differences in the operating systems to mismatches with JAR files and property settings. There also are database schemas, operating system settings, and many other settings in the environment to consider. An issue fixed in one environment will most likely occur in the next environment, and so on, until you are finally in production. It can be an extremely frustrating comedy of errors that repeats itself, no matter which company you go to. I often see managers shaking their heads in disbelief when they see the same errors move from one environment to another. They know the issues are going to come up again and again, but they just don't know what to do. For the most part, managers keep the key players who know the application and hope that those people stay around long enough to see the code moved from one environment to another, which can be a time-consuming process. It can take countless hours to get the environment right.

There are so many different settings in the environment that I am not surprised that problems occur. Engineers, however, tend to either ignore the problems or assume that the developers are looking at log files and making the necessary changes. (Most likely, they are not.) I think success in building and deploying these systems can be defined as the ability to minimize the impacts of a system being down by excellent communication and, ultimately, full automation of the deployment process. As you build these systems, always consider where automation may help with the process; then you will know that the next time a particular problem happens, it will be in another area and not in the one you just fixed.

Lock Down the Environment

Once the code is written, most of your time will be spent getting the code into your environments. One way to make sure that the environmental changes are not part of the application code is to separate the environment settings from the application code and lock down the environment. A locked down environment gives more repeatable results, and you can easily promote the build from one environment to another without having to change property files. How this is done is really up to you, but if possible, keep properties in a database. You might have a management console that allows you to make changes to the database. For many applications this just isn't feasible. Consider versioning of properties files to ensure that when an application goes into an environment, the last thing you would need to suspect would be an improper property file. You can also override the properties as system settings, instead of keeping the properties in the build. Some people keep all of the property files for each of the environments in source control. A flag is set for the environment to which you are pushing code. As long as you don't make a change to the environment settings, you will have the same results when you push code. Now, you can focus on the code issues, not the properties that cause the environmental issues.

Repeatable Results

To have a reliable environment, you must have repeatable processes that yield consistent results. This sounds like a very simple concept, but it's common for businesses to not have this process matured before going to production. A project manager will find it difficult to plan around inconsistent results from the code that was deployed; the process is not something you can plan around. The code issue may take one day or two weeks to resolve, which leads to frustration and wasting dollars. When dealing with the enterprise, it can be even trickier to have a repeatable process with consistent results. The solutions to doing this success-fully have all been to use automation to deploy code into environments. To have repeatable results, you need to make sure your code base is stable. Are you able to roll back to the last build? Do you have all of your code versioned? All of these steps add additional overhead and will cost more to maintain. So, based on your business requirements and how much money you can afford to lose, the answer depends on the amount of risk you want to take. Must you have a source control system? No. You can build from the trunk or base each time and deploy, but this is extremely risky. If you bet on never needing the backup and then something happens, you could easily be out of business. We also can get repeatable results by adopting a good configuration-management strategy. This ultimately will rely on the project team's willingness to adopt the new process and their taking ownership when there are issues. You want them to ask themselves, "How can we be part of the solution?" rather than thinking, "It's somebody's problem, but it's not mine."

Automation

Automation is imperative when you are trying to manage your environments. The larger the environment, the more automation you should have in place. It will take time to automate your application, but it is worth it in the long run. I don't have a preference for a particular way to automate; just make sure that it gets done and that it can be done with everything. You can automate any task that an engineer must manually perform. This includes Web server configuration, application server configuration, and just about anything else. Start automating the tasks that you find yourself repeating over and over again. You can include automating the build, rolling log files, deleting file caches—just about anything. Make sure that the task you are automating will have some value. If it is going to take you longer to automate it than the benefit you will get, then don't automate the process. If, however, you see someone spending a long time on things that you could have done in five minutes, it may be worth automating. A UNIX system, in my opinion, is easier to automate than a Windows environment.

Another common area to automate is the deployment of the code to the various environments. Developers regularly build code—this isn't anything new. They may not have to worry much about getting the code into the local environment, but the challenge comes when they need to get the code moved into the other environments. Adding the deployment at build time allows you to consistently deliver code to the environments. Once you have a repeatable build process, you can start to rule out issues with the build or missing a configuration step. This saves time, and the more time you save, the more time you have to focus on the core tasks at hand. Once you have an automated, repeatable build, focus on automating the starting and stopping of the servers. WebLogic console works great for smaller clusters; but I have seen the servers run into problems once there are more than twenty-eight servers per domain. In addition, it may be very time consuming to log into the console to determine the problems on the servers. The easiest way to do this is to automate the management of servers.

Now when you have an outage that requires all of the servers to be restarted, you can do so in minutes—not hours.

Labor is one of the expensive resources in business. We are all good at what we do, but we are still prone to error—I know that I am. But when I automate, I know the system will work as designed. It may occasionally fail, but when it does, I simply fix the issue and move on.

Plan

The best way to mitigate the environment issues is to plan for each deployment and change to the environment. Each stakeholder should be responsible for his own portion of the application. You will need to have a repeatable process that keeps the environment in place. One of the biggest issues I regularly encounter is an environment misconfiguration that leads to a production outage. Maintaining an environment on a small scale is relatively easy; issues usually occur more frequently when the environment starts growing. One of the more challenging and frustrating issues is planning for the time you'll need to thoroughly test the application to your satisfaction. Timelines are so tight—the business may be planning a promotion or letting the customer know that a key functionality is coming out. The business is so focused on what it knows and understands that it is really up to the technical folks to iterate the importance of the process. Planning is an important step in getting your process in place.

Implementation Plan

If you have a static application and no longer need to have code changes, you will not be pushing code very often. This is fine; there are plenty of applications that are pushed once and then forgotten until it's time for a change. When you do code deployments, however, you will want to be as efficient at pushing the code as possible. The way to do this is to have a solid implementation plan. The implementation plan provides a controlled way of getting the environment built out and code deployed. A well-documented implementation plan should point out the environment's key settings. This isn't limited to just the developers; this system should have input from all who have a hand in the system, including designers, developers, quality assurance, load testers, and administrators. An implementation plan is a contract of what steps need to be taken to get the build into production.

Always Have a Backup

In the real world, it has been said that only the paranoid survive; in an information world, the same can be said—with a slight variation: only those who backup their work will survive. One of the most important things you can do is to be obsessively compulsive about backing up your work. Never rely on someone else to do it for you, even when you do have a backup. Until the backup system has been tested, you can't rely on it.

For a music management application for a large company, I was the lead database administrator, application developer, and system administrator. There were many other components, however, that I did not own, including the storage area network (SAN), the network, and the system administration. I had an Oracle database, and each of the database files (DBF) was stored on a different SAN. Coming from a UNIX background, I think I developed better scripting habits. In UNIX, when a file is deleted, it is gone permanently, so I learned to constantly make backup files. One of the biggest fears I had was that a file would get deleted, and I would not have a backup. So, being paranoid about the backups, I would back up everything that I needed and placed it locally—just in case. On this music application, I took a backup every night and placed it on the local system disk. The systems administrators had assured me my data was safe, that I didn't need to waste the space on unnecessary backups. To make sure the data was backed up, one of the system administrators had to add the volumes to his nightly backup routines, which I assumed was done. After many meetings, I was assured that my data was safe.

One day at about 11:00 AM, I got an alert from my database—a script had automatically logged into the database, disconnected, and sent the result to a temporary file. The alert that the system sent to me was a standard database exception, which means that something happened on the database—but I didn't know what it was. I logged in and did a directory listing to show the disks, and the command hung up. This was bad—it meant that the command was unable to find disks. So I was either out of space on the disks, or they were gone altogether. I got one of the system administrators on the phone, and after a series of questions and probes, he admitted that all disks on the storage network had gone down. From the application view, the application was running, but it didn't have any disks to write to—not a good thing when the application relies on disks to run. I had no idea of what transactions had taken place or which ones were completed. I could only put up a "Site Down" page and get people off the system. At this point, my goal was to safely shut down the applications. I hoped that my data was intact when the SAN came back, so that I could recover the application data.

Several hours later, the SAN administrators had everything up and functioning. I restored my mount points and then started the database. But there was something wrong—the database didn't want to come up. I went though the database recovery process and found that I was missing a database file (DBF). Once the DBF is gone, the only choice is to run a backup. I called a SAN administrator to restore my data. After giving him the file name, I felt comfortable that my data would be restored. Once that was in place, a simple recovery would do the trick. But the engineer said that he didn't have that file in the index. Despite all the meetings and the assurance from the administrators, I was missing a key file to run my application. Without that file I could not get the database back up and running. I delivered the news that recovery might not be possible. I knew that I had a backup, but that was from the night before. I didn't know how much data I had lost.

It's important to manage expectations when it comes to issues. I'd rather give bad news first, and deliver good news later. I said that I was expecting a backup, but I was dead in the water until I was given one. Knowing that my strategy was to try a restore with my backup, I let the systems administrators sweat on the call while I staged the comeback. Management only knows what happens in production by reading the case notes from production outages. Take the time to clearly document the issues, make sure of them, and emphasize what is going on in situations like this. (In my situation, I repeated, several times, why the site was down.) If you don't have good documentation, you'll always be at fault for not doing something right. Try to gain control of the situation. Keep the conversation moving in a direction that is advantageous to getting the issues resolved.

After five minutes of letting management know that their processes had failed miserably, I announced I had one thing left to try. I couldn't guarantee it would work or the validity of the data, but it was worth a try. There is nothing more humbling than knowing that your process has failed, and an entire line of business needs to shut down because of the actions or nonactions on the part of one of the team members. I had already staged my backed-up file in the SAN, hoping the engineer didn't do a directory listing and find my backup. I felt even more confident because I knew the file that was missing contained static data, and last night's backup would be good enough. I ran my recover, and got the database back up and running. I tested all of the tables and started the application server. I was able to log in, and everything looked fine. I did some more sanity checking, just to make sure that this had fixed the issues. Then I announced that the application was running. The business would have to run through the application to make sure it was ready to be turned back on so customers could access it.

The business said it looked good, and I was asked about the resolution. Due to the file not getting into the backup index on the backup system, there wasn't a backup of the database file that I needed. I had to take a backup that I had made the night before and put it in its place. There is a science to this, but in this case, I just got lucky. As you can probably imagine, I never had another issue of a backup not being in the index on the backup system.

Source Control

Believe it or not, some large companies have written custom applications that are running in production, but they have lost the source code to those projects. These applications were developed by one or more of their employees, and now there is no way to change code, even if they wanted to. Fortunately for me, I have not been asked to re-create source code, because although I can think of a number of ways to do it, is it worth it? The bottom line is that you must have your code backed up and protected. The kind of repository you are using doesn't matter; it only matters that you are using one. Several source controls have hooks in them, so we can automate the checkout of the code before building the application. Source control could be an entire book in itself, so picking a good source control is out of the scope of this book.

Configuration Management

Building a J2EE application can be straightforward for simple applications. When your simple application needs to be integrated with other applications and have a common build-and-deploy strategy, the challenges with the application start to grow, and the scope of the application increases. It gets even more difficult if there are multiple developers working on systems, with multiple integrations and from different geographic regions. Managing the versioning of the builds becomes a full-time job to keep the process working. A lot of frustration can result from a poor configuration-management strategy; getting a solution in place is critical so your operational efficiencies can take place. A lot of symptoms can indicate a poor configuration management strategy—or the lack of one in place. Some of the telltale signs are e-mailing of JARs and class files from one developer to another, putting JARs on a shared drive, or inconsistent build results each time you need to get an application into an environment. The lack of control can go as far as applications that are running in production that serve a business function, but there is no record of the source code for the application.

Application Deployment

When should you deploy your application on one cluster with an application on it, rather than creating a new cluster for the application? This depends on the architecture and how the developers have built the application. There are so many valid ways to deploy an application; it really depends on how the application was written. When making the deployment, however, it is important to consider the strategy for managing your dynamic environment files, as well as how you plan to update those properties when you have a cluster. It's not only getting the properties in place; it is also important, once they are in place, to validate that the servers are configured correctly—there needs to be a way to validate the environment. For example, let's say you bundle an application together. You have a wireless application with which cell phones access and a wired application that customers access through a Web browser. One application is for the Web browser on your computer; the other is for the phone. When should you separate—or should you separate at all? What is the deciding factor? Even though it makes sense to separate due to performance requirements, you may also introduce issues early in production due to serving both applications from the same JVM.

Kitchen Sink JARs

A developer and those new to J2EE applications often get a common error message: "NoClassDefFoundError." A way to get rid of that error is to put the JAR (Java Archive) in the class path that contains the class—then the error goes away. New developers will sometimes add every possible JAR file to the class path to try to get rid of the errors. By doing this, they think they can get the application working and then go back to fix it later. Often, however, there is no time to go back to fix it, so this procedure can be the start of a bad habit. Unless you start with a disciplined and principled approach to packaging your applications, you will always be in a position where you need to clean it up. As you develop your application code and integrate components, think about the most effective way to work. Using a third-party component is about code reuse. It simply does not make sense to package the same JAR files, multiple times, in an application. Nor does it make sense to needlessly add jar files to the application hoping you get rid of an error. One of the key questions to ask your development teams is, "Do we have these issues in our build environments?"

The gatekeeper to the environments is the application administrator, and if you are in that role, it is important for you to identify the issues and bubble it up to the developers. Not only are they the gatekeepers for the code, but they should also make sure that you have the correct deployment. It is a simple matter to check on the applications, either through a checksum or a size validation of the application deployed. There are also ways you can modify the application JAR itself in the manifest and label it with the version number of the build. Be aware of the deployment directories and common files. The application administrators have firsthand knowledge on the environments and can make sure the deployment descriptors are set up correctly. This may be one of the places you will need to look when you get into trouble. You will need to spend a large amount of time working with the deployment descriptors for both the Web application and EJB servers. These files can cause numerous headaches if you are unsure of what you are looking at. The key to being successful with the deployment descriptors—and any setting, for that matter—is to get the changes put into the build process.

Minimize the Footprint

Keep the deployment as small as possible. If an enterprise repository (EAR) is sharing resources with multiple applications, put the JAR files in a common area, such as APP-INF (a special directory inside an EAR file). It is far simpler to create the deployment correctly the first time than to later work through issues and irregularities caused by improper deployments. It is important to know what you are adding to your application and the reasons for doing so. Creating a build with additional JARs, just to get the application quickly to production, is careless and will cause problems in the future. If you see issues with JARs and how they are deployed, be sure to escalate to get these issues addressed early in the process, rather than waiting until it becomes an issue. The J2EE structure is fairly simple, but if you don't have a lot of experience with it and with the terminology, it can be a bit overwhelming. The newer IDEs, like WebLogic Workshop, make building robust business applications almost foolproof. They will take care of all the packaging and build scripts for you. If you follow their framework, you will comply with the J2EE specification. The applications are integrated with the application server and make developing enterprise-level code very easy. Working within existing frameworks will give you the best chance for success with your application structure. If, however, you are building a custom application that requires you to support multiple application servers, then your strategy would be different.

Text Editor

Getting the environment right is so critical to the operation of your applications. Once the code is written, at least 75 percent of the time is spent on getting the configuration right for production. Getting the environment created and built is pretty straightforward if you have an automated way to build the environments. The best-practices approach is to create an implementation plan, and do all your deployments off of that plan. In the real world, you may find a situation where there isn't an implementation plan, and the environments were built from memory and from the properties files that the company thinks belong in the environment. Invest in a good text editor with a good file and directory-comparison capabilities. Tools like ExamDiff Pro, Araxis Merge, or TextPad work well. With the number of property files, configuration files, and JARs for each environment; you need a tool that will quickly retrieve information on the differences in the environments. The time to resolution on issues will be greatly improved. Engineers also use such a tool to create the property files for the new environments. You cannot expect to find the differences if you jump into a new environment without a tool like a good text editor for comparison of your files.

Build the Application Locally

It is helpful to have a local instance of your application on your workstation. This takes a lot of additional time and resources, but it is helpful for a number of reasons including two in particular: it will increase your knowledge of the components and the other applications with which you are integrating; and it will give you an opportunity to troubleshoot issues without being dependent on others. Having your own local environment isn't always possible—some systems have hundreds of components—but if you are able to have a local instance, you can improve your chances of success with the application. I like to have a local instance so I can point to all of the authorized back-ends. By doing so, I can experiment with deployment descriptors' performance settings and debug patches without impeding the release. In addition to familiarizing yourself with all the components, I think the real value to having a local instance is in getting a 360-degree view of the application. Companies tend to create specialists in one area. If you get a detailed understanding of how all the components fit together, you will know the application better than others do. This is one of the ways you build breadth of knowledge. It is important not only to understand the area you are focusing on but also the systems and components you are dependent on.

Automate Builds

The automation of the builds can be done any number of ways. The most common is to have a scripting language, such as Ant or Maven (these are two common open source build tools), which builds and deploys the applications for you. Ant can also help you manage your properties files and deploy the code. I cannot underscore enough the importance of having a consistent build process. When you expect consistent results, you must make sure there is consistency in the environment—in the build process and in the development practices you use on a daily basis. Having the code quickly deployed to an environment is important. However, it is not enough to know how to deploy the code quickly that is important. You also need to know which version of the code is in each of the environments and be able to ensure consistency with the deployment process. You need to feel confident that when you push the button to deploy, the same code and configuration files get pushed to the environment correctly. It is just as important as having your environmental settings checked into a source-control system. Checking environment-specific settings into a source-control repository gives access to everyone so that they have the ability to review the settings in production without having to look in production.

I've found Ant to be the most common deployment tool. It's a fairly simple markup language that allows you to create automation scripts. You don't have to worry about moving it from machine to machine. You can set up properties files that are read at run time—the language runs through an Ant interpreter. With Ant, you can quickly get your build scripts ready and usable, without having to follow too many steps. Ant also has many optional tasks that you can use to deploy files to your application server, as well as several other options for getting your code to production.

You will see more advanced scripts that have all of the property file settings for environments. When you run your builds, you specify the environment for which you are building and run the Ant command. Build scripts are typically created by the developer, but any savvy system administrator should be able to update, modify, and maintain them. The most sophisticated example I have seen of a build script was one that built a custom Web application on top of the Ant scripts. It was possible to control which build to push (and to which environment) through a user interface. This process of automating the builds and getting code and environment settings to that environment is really what gaining stability in the environment is all about. Once you have determined what is needed to get to each of the environments, getting the Ant scripts in place is straightforward. You will automate the process you are already manually doing. The hard part is identifying the manual steps to get the environment built out right the first time. And one of the hardest parts is in getting an environment set up with all the right property files and locking down the code.

Configuration management may take on a number of roles. The configuration manager becomes the gatekeeper for the environments. He is someone who is called upon when you need to control what gets pushed into the environments and when. The configuration manager may handle the merges from one branch to another. He may write or aggregate the build scripts for a certain application. He may be responsible for all of the environment variables and ensure that they get propagated from one environment to another. The goal of the configuration-management process extends past the source control and property files; it may also include project documentation-implementation plans and whatever other artifacts are needed to promote these builds from one environment to another. Tools vary, depending on the job, but they include a source-control repository. They need a scripting language to be able to manage property files and create deployment files for the various environments.

Automate Your Environment

The larger your application-server farm gets, the more important it is to find a strategy to manage the farm with a limited number of resources. Some companies have upward of four thousand application servers in their environments. With that number of servers to manage, there must be a strategy in place to handle the servers. For argument's sake let's say we are going to set up a large cluster of application servers. The cluster will have sixty servers—forty presentation and twenty back-end servers—to handle the business rules and data access. Just think about this problem, how are you going to install, develop, and configure all these servers without a large group of people or automation? If you don't have an infinite number of resources to dedicate, the solution has to be automation. I was the team leader of a load-test effort, and we were in the final phase of load testing and getting ready for production. The load test was going terribly; there were errors all over the place. There was going to be a recycle of the servers, so I figured there would be a fifteen-minute break. We contacted the support; they said they'd made some configuration changes and needed to have the servers bounced. This sounded like an easy request, and I asked how long it would take, assuming we would be ready to go in fifteen minutes. After a pause, I was told that it would take about two hours. When I asked why it would take so long, the support person said that I would need to log into all sixty servers and restart them.

In large systems, millions of dollars in transactions go through in an hour. In production, we would have lost at least twenty million dollars in unrecoverable revenue. We waited the two hours that night for all the servers to come up. Two hours went by—but nothing happened. I checked back with the engineer; he had been pulled off to work on something else.

"I have a solution," I told him.

"I won't have time to implement it," he told me.

"Let me do it for you," I offered.

I got no response from him. Finally, five hours later, he got the environment up and running.

I liked the engineer, but I felt I had to escalate this issue to his manager the next day. Here was a guy who was doing everything he could to jump in to get the job done. And while I respected him for that, there was no reason to needlessly waste company resources when there was a better way to do the job. If you have a better solution that will save time, I would encourage you to get it out in the open and up for discussion. Later that week I showed the engineer the script to save time restarting all the servers and helped implement it; it took about half a day to write and set up on the servers. The script killed the servers and got the server up and running in about ten minutes. I had some little issues to work out with the script, but for the most part, a five-hour job manual job was done in ten minutes with a script.

Cluster Early

Getting a system to mimic production early on in the environments is a must if you want to have a smooth transition to production. To successfully develop a cluster-ready application, you need to write cluster-aware code. I'm sure that if you adopt this strategy early on in the development cycles, you will find and resolve issues before you get to production. If you are running into intermittent errors on the site and the application seems to work fine in a stand-alone environment, then check how the developers implemented their cluster-aware code. A common symptom of code that is not cluster aware is when you are logged into a site, you click on a button or link, and you are automatically redirected to a log-in page. Something may have happened to your server's session, and now you are being failed over to a server that does not have your backup session on it. This isn't the only reason for this type of behavior, but it is indicative of some of the issues you may run into when you are working with applications. Go back and question the development and integration environments. Did you have a clustering setup? Were these issues brought up before in this environment but perhaps were ignored? If you have any requirements for high availability of your systems, you cannot afford to miss this step. Make sure you test the cluster early by building test cases to simulate the server going down and your finding out what happened to the data. Also, consider testing multiple failure scenarios. Look back to determine all the points where the application can fail. Simulate the failure, and document what happened. Was the system successfully able to handle and recover from the issue, or did it fail? If you do not cluster in your development environments you will ultimately run into cluster issues in another environment.

Document the Application

A hundred-million-dollar project once never made it to production because of many issues discussed in this book. I was brought in late in the process to help the performance team. While I was there, they assigned a new manager to the team. The team members knew about all aspects of the application, and one day, the new manager brought up documentation. The application had several hundred developers writing code for it. The manager turned to one of the engineers.

"Documentation was lacking on the applications," the manager said.

"Yes," the engineer confirmed, "documentation was light. The team could have done a better job."

"Your next assignment," the manager then said, "is to document the application."

It was hard for me to keep a straight face when I heard this. I knew that this engineer had quite a temper, and I knew what would happen next.

"Do you realize that this is a large application?" the engineer asked the manager. "Documentation could take some time."

A rather heated debate followed, and I don't think the manager was ever able to get back the respect he needed to be effective at his job. In fact, the manager left for another position.

There is no doubt that the application needed to be documented, but you set yourself up for failure and cost the company money if you make requests that can never be accomplished. You need to be honest with these requests. Unless you have extremely technical managers, a manager will just manage resources and may not understand the complexity of a task such as documentation. To get the proper documentation on the application, you need to have that built into the process. One person can be responsible for getting documentation. It is highly unlikely that he will be successful, unless there is a process to get the documentation in place, and a system to maintain it. If you are surrounded by management that makes suggestions like "document the application," you will be doomed to failure. There is a good chance that the application won't make it to production anyway. In the above situation, I think the manager was in over his head. A good manager would have compromised and come to win-win understanding on what was essential to document and who the intended audience was for this document.

Targeted Training

As an engineer or manager, you send your people to training—have a training manual for your application. The same holds true for your custom applications. Without tailored training for your application, transition can be difficult. I think it is great to have a custom training manual for a custom application. It can be quite challenging to build the application as fast as possible, while trying to document that application. And even though you have robust documentation, people rarely read it. Then it's often the case that the documentation doesn't get updated frequently, so you end up with documentation that is not usable. When you order a training class from a vendor, always ask to have it customized. I like training classes, but I don't have a lot of time. The best use of my training dollars is to get a focused class that meets the business needs. From a practical perspective, you can save money when you combine two classes. Have the vendor focus on the key issues you are facing. Many companies do not have enough resources to allow their employees to attend classes all day, especially if they are actively supporting applications. If you have the ability to break up the class into shorter sessions, people will get the most out of it. Remember: if you do not manage the classes and environments, they will end up managing you.

LOAD TESTING FOR SUCCESS

One of the most commonly overlooked areas is the load test. The number of enterprises with problems that regularly recycle servers to fix issues would concern the best technical minds. You may have in-flight transactions, and at any point, a server may be recycled and force live customers off the site. Many of these issues can be fixed if caught early in the load-test cycle, and they must be resolved before the application goes to production. Load testing is a complicated effort that takes a very skilled technical lead that can identify all of the key components. I have been involved in numerous load-test efforts and have driven the test plans through to execution. Of the many tests I have run, I have never seen one that 100 percent directly emulated what production load would look like. The best that you can do is to approximate the expected load and hope it is a good enough educated guess at best. The pitfalls are endless and range from not having enough agents to not propagating all environmental changes to the environment. The problems are compounded when you poorly defined process, and there are difficulties getting the applications into the new environment. Load testing is not easy. Some companies give up on load-test efforts because they cannot get successful results or because management decides it's a one-time test. They may even cut the budget on testing before going live with their systems, which just isn't practical. I often see acceptance of load-test results that are essentially fabricated—or might as well be, given the test cases and inability of the teams to produce results.

Load-Test Basics

Load testing can be as simple as setting up a couple of servers and hitting them with a couple of users and one test case. Most load-test efforts, however, are a bit more complex. In an enterprise, this may run into millions of dollars. While I can't cover all the pitfalls associated with load testing, I can share my experience to keep you from running into the major issues.

Determine What You Are Going to Test

Before you can start a load test, you must identify what you want to get out of it. What information are you trying to get from the load test? Once you have a goal, you can start to plan for your load test. How do you know if the load test was successful? When are you finished with load testing? There are some applications where load testing is simple; it can be done with relative ease. With the applications I've work on however, this has very rarely been the case. The larger the project, the more overruns in development, and the more time constraints are placed on load testing. You are at a disadvantage when implementing new applications that have no history. If you overestimate the production load, your system will be ready when your load increases. If you do not plan on enough requests, or if the business requests are different from what you expected, look out—you either will be able to quickly fix the issues and move on, or you will fail miserably.

Customer-Usage Patterns

Predicting how a customer is going to use a Web site or Web service is difficult to do, but one of the simplest ways is to break down the application by business-use cases. Calculate the frequency of the use cases, and script them independently. Then run them in parallel at the rate you would expect the use cases to happen in production. If the application is a replacement of an existing system, then you should know the usage patterns. You can run a load test, and run a hits monitor against your Web logs to see if you can find patterns between production results and the load-test environments. In any case, it isn't easy to predict the load, and it is even harder to get an accurate representation of the load on the servers. Just do the best you can, and be creative. If you've had experience with servers in the past, you should be able to predict where the server will have issues.

Generating the Load

A big mistake when load testing is to take applications that will handle millions of unique log-ins per day, and load test with only one load-generation device. Load tests can be invalid due to the number of requests a load tool is trying to simulate. Many claim they can use hundreds, if not thousands, of simultaneous users, and it may make sense from a budget perspective, but this just does not work from a practical perspective. In reality, will a system handle the load from thousands of users from only one agent? The bottleneck in the load generation is that a single CPU (Central Processing Unit) machine with one network card is not able to handle the load. It isn't possible, and you will encounter numerous issues just trying to get this to work. Another issue is making sure the load is evenly load-balanced across servers. Load testing is performed to try to simulate thousands of users in a mock environment. This challenge can seem daunting—it seems almost an impossible task to try to simulate every customer click and simulate peak periods. A key factor to make sure you are simulating the proper traffic patterns is to do IP spoofing (simulate load coming from multiple IP addresses). When you have all the IP addresses coming in from a single node, you will see that the session is piling up on one server, and the rest are idle.

The load-generation tools range from a simple request from a browser to complex load-testing tools with multiple agents and controllers that drive load to your applications. The Grinder is a simple tool you can use to drive load to your environment. This is a free tool, compared to Segue, Load Runner, and a variety of other tools that are not free but used frequently in the enterprise environments. In some situations in an enterprise-application testing, the Grinder tool can be useful when you need to quickly test a component and don't have the resources or time to go through a formal load-test plan.

Developers can also write their own programs to hit the servers, if you prefer, and simulate load on the system. They will write a tool that calls their application multiple times, and it will time the result. It is very simple, but it is a load test, and a system your developers should understand that methods with lots of overhead that can cause issues. Regardless of the form of load testing you do, formal or not, you need a good understanding of how that application will do in production. The more experienced you are with performance, the better you'll be able to predict the behavior of the application. But until you are able to do that, load testing is an absolute must.

Load-Test Goals

Performance tuning is (or should be) done in the load-test environments, which are, by far, the most difficult to set up and configure of any of the environments. Not only is there the challenges of setting up the environments, but there also are multiple other factors. I think the biggest one is that with the environment and load testing. We are trying to simulate what the production will look like and that is hard to do. The load testing takes many forms and is normally conducted based on the test plan. Tests that are critical to the success of the application are the following: the performance test and the destructive test. When you perform tests in these areas, you'll get a better idea of how to predict how the application is going to perform once you deploy to production. Performance can take on three core tests cycles: peak capacity, longevity, and max performance. The destructive test is used to determine how the applications will perform when one or more components of the application fails.

Achieving the best performance of applications requires a combination of tests to determine the best overall configuration for your application. What is the best performance our application can produce without going to back-end systems? What is our performance if we lose a disk? What is the performance at peak load of the system? What happens to the system when doing an incremental backup of the database? These and more questions can all be answered during the load test. There are a lot of ways you can test. The more experience you have running these applications the more it can give you the answers you need.

During load testing you will run various scenarios—for example, a peak-performance test, a full twenty-four-hour test, or a one-week test. The test plan will identify the criteria needed to successfully pass the load test, and you'll work to achieve those objectives. These load tests require the coordination of multiple departments and requires much more support to run. In this scenario, you are using a live back-end with real data. You may encounter several issues that could be due to network configuration code. Once you have the test identified and a test plan prepared, you will use a load-generation suite to take in your use case and multiply it by one hundred or two hundred and then hit the servers. The main goal is to see what the code is doing and how your code can handle the required load. You can also derive the capacity of a system; identify memory leaks and many other issues. I have outlined some of the common tests below, there are other tests you can do such as capacity but these tests are some that I feel important when getting ready for production.

Regardless of the type of load you are running, a difficult challenge is to ensure the load you are putting on the servers is an accurate representation of what is going to be in production. Use the JMX monitoring tools to get metrics on sessions, thread utilization memory, and other components to determine if the load is accurate. For example, I have seen load tests where they seemingly have performance issues during the load test. I am assured the load test is valid and that there are no issues with the test. How many users do you expect? Let's say for argument's sake 1,000 total users and 25 users per hour. Looking back at the sessions on the servers after a one-hour test I see 4,000 sessions created. The argument is invariably the same every time; well they are going to be doing multiple transactions. That is fine but you should have 25 sessions, maintain affinity to those 25 sessions and then create transactions to equal the expected load under each of the sessions.

Bench Test: In a development environment, the developer introspects his code and looks for performance issues.
Goal: Identify performance issues early on in the process.

Performance Test: In a stand-alone environment with the back-end stubbed, how fast will the application's code run?
Goal: Identify the performance bottlenecks in the code upfront, and quickly move back into the development cycle.

Endurance Test: How long can you sustain load on your servers?
Goal: Determine the peak load you can handle. Determine how long it will take to crash the server.

Destructive Test: When you bring down certain components, how long can your application work?
Goal: Test your dependencies, and predict the results when key components fail.

Bench Test

The first experience an application has with performance testing takes place when the developer writes the code. Use critical thinking: is this the best way to write the code? The developer should be able to predict any performance implications at this stage. A good developer will know the consequences of his actions and be able to take the path of least resistance. If I am retrieving data from a database and there are 7,000K records, does it make sense to show all those records? Some people might review those records in a single sitting in a Web application, but that seems unlikely. The bench test can be as simple as putting in some timers to debug the applications or use a profiling tool that looks at the code on a very detailed level. Profilers are beneficial because they help the developer understand, from another perspective, how many resources the system is using. The developer looks at the code at a microlevel, understanding how all the code impacts memory and, to some degree, the CPU. Impacting memory is obvious—it depends on the size of the objects I am creating. The CPU is a factor because of the number of threads I need to get the job done.

You can also use JUNIT testing, a regression testing tool for developers, to test the code before sending the load through the systems to ensure the code is functional. The test case which may or may not be related to the load scenario will keep you from manually having to test the application to ensure the application is working as designed. These tools can be very helpful in the development cycles. When there is a change in code, I can quickly regression-test the application so that I know the impact of the change before the code is pushed to production.

Performance Test

The performance test is run in a disconnected environment, usually during the development process. As you write code, you will create a test plan, and test those individual units as they are developed. It is assumed that with this test, there is no back-end system, and all components will be available at all times. So you can send incredible amounts of load to the system to just test the core components. The goal with this test is to identify how long it takes, with stubbed data, for the code to execute. This is also a good time to look for duplicate method calls and any issues that you may not be able to see running in the bench test. You can use the Grinder or any other open-source utility to test applications. The load-test efforts, at this point, may not be very well defined, and it is difficult to get a solid service-level agreement from the business. Pick the most common component test, and make them run as fast as you can. This part of load testing can get frustrating. You may not have code completion, and functionality may be missing, but you have to start somewhere. The requirement for having a good performance test is to stub out the back-end business logic. You aren't testing the database or other dependent systems; in a lot of cases, you're testing the business logic and presentation layer. During this phase, load testing is not going to be much fun—in fact, there is often more frustration than accomplishment.

Endurance Test

Endurance testing is used to identify any memory leaks or, to put it more correctly, collection of unnecessary objects. Over time—say, twenty-four hours, forty-eight hours, or perhaps a week of testing—how do your application servers handle the consistent load pushed to the system? The key metrics you need to understand are which resources are being used and whether they are returned to the application server for garbage collection. It's been my experience that this test is the one most often omitted when doing load testing. One of the main reasons for this is that by the time the testing team gets the application and finally gets the load test working in the environment, they may already be behind schedule with the application. By the time they get ready to do the endurance test, there is no time to complete the activity. If you have to omit the endurance test, make sure you keep a close eye on memory allocation in production.

Destructive Testing

Destructive testing is used to identify what happens to the system when one or more components are shut down during the load test. You want to know the state of your transactions, but more importantly, you want to know about the customer experience. Building a test plan for destructive testing varies, but the basic questions you need to answer are "What can fail?" and "How will we simulate that failure when servers are running and in the middle of a load?" You can also failover the database at some point and sometimes kill networks, firewalls, and so forth. You can also test disaster recovery at this point. What is the impact to your users if you are forced to restore a system in the middle of the day? With these various scenarios of load testing, you can learn a lot from your servers and environment. This is a great time to get to know the new application before it goes to production. It is your job to look for warning signs. Several enterprise test applications have been checked from top to bottom but still fail in production.

Common Issues in Load Test

There are numerous issues that you can run into during the load testing of an application. Setting up the environment may be as difficult as setting up production or any other environment. The biggest challenge, as I see it, is being able to generate the load and synthesize all the user interactions. The best advice I can give is to have an open mind. I will document the most common pitfalls that I've encountered, and I hope that you will be able to plan around them—and then you won't have sleepless nights in the weeks after your implementation. One of the most common issues is related to the environment setup and the environmental settings that are required to run the system. If possible, get new hardware that eventually will be part of the production environment. Shaking out an environment can be difficult; if you have the opportunity to use the load-test hardware for production, it will make things easier.

Production Load Test

Your load testing should not stop after you go to production. Production is the environment for which you build the code, and it's the most accurate representation of what your load-test load should have looked like. Now, before you start pointing your load-generation tools to the production environment, let me clarify: the best load-test tool is the users of the system. Find a way to get metrics once you get into production. Monitor the system for poor-performing areas after the code has been deployed and you are actively using the system. Maybe load testing is not the best way to look at this effort, but you should always be monitoring the system for performance. Load testing is one way to do this so that it is noninvasive to the end user. Once you get into production, whether you like it or not, load is going to be driven to the system. Having the ability to capture the errors and exceptions that take place in production is the best way to move toward continuous improvement.

Lessons Learned

There are numerous settings in an environment. You must monitor system settings, database settings, network settings, application settings, and application-server settings. The key is to always propagate the lessons learned in an environment back to the project teams. It is a constant movement of data in environments—different groups will run development, integration, system test, load test, and production. It seems like a fairly simple concept, but it often can cause several issues. You will find—more often than not—that teams do not learn from their mistakes. They work through the same issues in each of the environments. The integration team goes through the pain of getting the application deployed and has no choice but to get a developer involved. The integration team then deploys the same issue to another environment. The developer gets involved again, to get it into the environment. This process happens for each of the environments. At some point, you would think that release notes would be mandatory to identify the issues and document them. Learning lessons in environments and getting those back into the process is crucial to gaining control over deployments.

Identify Issues

Issues always result from load-testing efforts that go unnoticed. It is wrong to assume that the development environment or production will be much more stable. More attention should have been given to evaluating the issues and reviewing log files. Some exceptions will show up in the production implementation that could have been fixed in another environment. While environmental problems do account for some of the issues, they are certainly not all of them. This is why you should use an iterative approach to solving these problems. A constant stream of data is pushed back from the environments to the developers and, ultimately, into the next releases. When you can identify these issues quickly and get them fixed, the load-testing efforts will go much better. To be able to really dig into the exceptions, however, and to understand why those error messages were received, takes the coordination of all involved. You may be surprised to discover that your issues are solvable. The developer may have no idea that a situation found in the test environment could be a valid path for the code. If you do your research and get the data back to the developers, the product will get better. As a result, your time will be more productive, and the company will be better able to compete with those companies that have the better processes in place.

Load-Test Process

Why do these applications fail in production? They went through all the steps of testing. Things should be okay. Things probably went a lot better due to the testing than not performing any tests. You may have poorly trained administrators and personnel who are new to testing and who do not know what to look for. It really isn't any one person's fault. The fault usually lies with management for not hiring the right resources or not putting enough of a priority on an issue. If you are an absentee manager and do not spend the time to get to know the issues, you will definitely get to know them when production comes around. Take the time to get a technical resource to take accountability for the environments. Hire a consultant who specializes in this area—this is critical to ensure that you are ready when it is time to launch the application for the first time. Load testing is a process, and it doesn't happen overnight or after one load test. If you don't have the right people looking at the right places while the load test is going on, you might as well not run it. Running it will only get you into more trouble and keep you from doing what is important: getting the applications written and to production.

COMMON AREAS TO WATCH OUT FOR

This chapter identifies the common areas where you may find performance issues in the enterprise environment. It is by no means all-inclusive, but it covers, more or less, some of the key issues with which I have worked over the years. I think the key with these pitfalls is that over time, you want to be able to predict when these issues will impact you so you can get these into your design before they become an issue.

Remote Calls

When making a remote call, keep in mind that the remote call will consume resources of the system. In a Java application server, you use a thread to wait for that resource and a socket on the operating system, which translates into an additional connection through the firewall. Remote calls can also cause additional network traffic if they are not designed properly. Remote calls have the disadvantage of overhead, of getting the remote connection. Be very cautious with any code that calls external resources. It is not just a matter of whether to release the resource but whether you also have a time-out in place to release the resource, in the event that the remote resource doesn't respond. You also should be concerned with how often you are going to call a remote call and how much data you will get back. Be very aware of how fine grained your remote calls are. If you keep them too fine grained, you can bog down the network or servers with the amount of times you need to go to the back-end system for more data.

Deployment Descriptors

Given that the container or application servers has its own set of configuration files called deployment descriptors, you need to be extremely cognizant of what they are and how they can impact the performance of your application. An application that runs perfectly fine in development and in test environments may not work in production. The deployment descriptors are a way to tell the container how to behave. When you change a deployment descriptor you tell the container how to behave differently. Be careful when making modifications to the deployment descriptors. If you make changes without knowing the consequences, you may introduce a performance issue, just by making the change.

Session Replication

Data may not be as predictable in production as you saw it in development, which may translate into the size of your session objects. The session objects are objects that contain data you use to store state (save the user session) on the server. You will most likely keep the user name and password, some preferences, and, depending on the requirement, a whole range of other data sets. Session replication is when you take the session or state of a user on Server A and make a copy of that session for failover purpose. The idea is that if a user is logged on to a machine and it goes down, he can resume work on Server B without having to reauthenticate or lose the non-transient data before it is persisted to disk or database. When you move the application from a development environment, which has a small set of test data, into production, where the data may be ten times the size of the test, you may run into problems. The way the application is used may be different when you use it in production. Production may have sessions that are several megabytes in size. The challenge to understand is how your code is handling these large sets of data coming back from database or downstream systems. Let's say you do a search and bring back a list of six hundred records. If persistence is on, this object is stored in session, and then the application server will replicate the data to another node in case of failure. Now, six hundred records may sound like a lot, but the process of serializing and sending them across to another node in the cluster does take some time and resources. You need to be aware of the data that is transient and can be thrown away, as well as what you need to persist (save) in the near and long term.

Deployment Scripts

If you plan to keep an environment for any period of time, you will most likely want to automate how you get code into that environment. Having a repeatable process will better assure your chances of success when it comes time to deploy code; not automating the environment will cause inconsistent results. Review deployment scripts, and make sure you have redundancy in the process. You also will need to account for errors and, if possible, back up the code and any other artifacts prior to deploying the new code and or scripts. Deployments happen at all hours of the day and night—doing a deployment in the middle of the night has its own challenges, but add a full day of work the day before to your being tired, and you can make all sorts of mistakes. When you determine your best-practices approach for dealing with the clusters, keep in mind the growth and the possibility—you may need to add additional servers to support the growth of the company and/or applications.

Automate Troubleshooting

Automating your deployment makes a lot of sense, and if you are considering it, why not automate the troubleshooting process as well? Business applications are constantly evolving, and even the best developers may introduce a code bug from time to time, or you may run into an issue that you never could have predicted. So once you have defined a process that works to gather information from your servers, try automating the way you collect and categorize the data.

Load Balancers

When looking at the load-balancing, I take a simplistic approach. Depending on the application, it may be preferable to use a hardware load balancer instead of a software level load balancer. The simple solution works for 80 percent of the applications, but there are always exceptions, and I deal with them as I run into them. Load balancing is very common among *n*-tier applications, and it is more common to have a load balancer than not. If you are going to use a load balancer, you need to understand a couple of key concepts that are not always well documented. Making the wrong decision with the load balancer can cost you performance.

There are basically two different types of load balancers: a software-level load balancer and a hardware load balancer. The hardware load balancers (hardware appliance) most commonly route based on the IP addresses, so for a hardware-level load balancer to know where to send a particular packet, it only has to go to the third layer in the TCP/IP stack before it knows what to do with the request. The software-level load balancer must move up into the application layer to determine where it needs to send the request. This may be based on a cookie header. The main difference is usually that the hardware load balancer is a dedicated appliance used to route the traffic. The software load balancer is a plug-in on the Web servers and shares components with the Web servers. When you plan your load-balancing strategy, here are a few things to keep in mind.

In your design, the additional overhead caused by checking the TCP/IP packet at the seventh layer of the OSI model will consume more resources. In general, a hardware-level load balancer may be faster with network traffic. That is not always the case, however, when the requirement is to route based on data in the header of the request. You can use the hardware load balancer to route more intelligently at a higher level, but it is not configured to do that out of the box. I am specifically talking about routing the JSESSIONID, which is a Java session identifier that is generated on the application server. Another alternative for hardware is to use a software level cookie the hardware application generates.

A software-level load balancer is an application-level load balancer. It does the routing based on the unique identifier that the application server has generated, such as a cookie store in the request header. The benefit of using this approach is that the software plug-ins will know where your session is and they bind that connection to the application server. In general, for http requests I find that the software load balancers work better at handling the traffic than the hardware-level load balancers; that is, in the majority of the situations, the benefits of using the software-level load balancer outweigh the detriments of not using it. I am not advocating using software-level load balancers all the time, but there are situations when you have lot of stateless requests, and the additional overhead to maintain an affinity or relationship with one server would be costly. Deciding when to use software-level rather than hardware-level really should be based on the application you are designing. Sometimes, you will not know the right approach until you have had time to load test the applications. For the most part, though, I usually end up going with a hybrid approach—a combination of hardware and software-level load balancing.

Affinity

Affinity is the relationship or kinship between two entities. The affinity, as it relates to the application server, is the relationship between the client and the servers over the life of the session. Each client creates a session with the server, and he keeps that relationship until the death of the session. When you put a hardware load balancer in place, the load balancer typically does not respect that affinity and may match the client to the server based on the IP address. This affinity at the hardware level is also called "sticky", which I will discuss in the next section. You can define the affinity based on a number of factors, but the two most common relationships are at the IP level or at the application level, such as the session ID or cookie. Load balancers have the ability to interact at the application level and can keep with a cookie, but it works best at Level 3. In my experience I can program a load balancer to bind based on data in the headers, but it does cause a lot of additional overhead on the load balancer appliance. In contrast, a proxy plug-in is a software-level load balancer that works at the application level. There is additional overhead caused by the proxy plug-in, but for the most part, you would deploy it on a dedicated Web server, and Web servers usually serve static data and can afford the additional overhead.

Sticky

Sticky is the relationship between the load balancer and the back-end server to which the load balancer is routing. The sticky relationship comes into play when a client comes to the load balancer, and the load balancer makes a relationship between the Java applications servers based on the source IP address of the client. For Internet applications, this may not present a problem, but when you have entire call centers coming from a proxy server that appears to be one address, the relationship from all clients inside the call center are routed to one server in the cluster. If one server goes down, an entire call center may be out of luck. Understanding how the applications will get to your applications is just as important when setting up the application configuration. A solution that works great in an Internet may not work so well when you are inside the firewall. This is complicated when you have call centers that deal with specific businesses that may use more server resources than others. An example may be a billing department. It must research billing issues, and these billing-related questions may require a lot of data. Now, all the traffic will go to one server in the cluster, and the rest of the servers are underutilized. You can check if this is an issue in your organization by looking at the way the application is load balancing across the servers in the cluster. Another indicator is when an entire data center is bound to one application server, when there may be ten to choose from. If this is the case, consider revisiting the load-balancing strategy to help better distribute the traffic across all servers in the cluster.

EJB Load Balancing versus Servlet

Much of the load balancing I've discussed is for the http traffic. There is a subtle difference when you load balance an RMI (Remote Method Invocation) call instead of a regular http. The following example is specific to WebLogic: after you get your initial context, the cluster will broadcast back the address on which to return the call. This is a little different from the http traffic request and can cause some issues. My experience with the load balancer and EJBs is that load balancing works great for the initial load balancing, but subsequent requests may go directly to the server and bypass the load balancer. Keep this in mind when you set up load balancing for your EJB layers. Another way to handle load balancing is to create DNS names for the servers that will participate in the cluster. The DNS name maps to a comma-separated list of IP addresses of the servers that are going to participate in the cluster.

Dynamic versus Static Content

One key way to dramatically improve your Java application server performance is to differentiate the dynamic content from the static content. But can't an application server also serve static content? Yes, that is true, but at what cost? The cost is usually performance when you are working with high-traffic applications. In some cases, it may make sense to serve images from the application server. To build a robust n-tier application, it is important to separate roles and responsibilities among the various components to scale the application most effectively. Serving static content for very high-volume sites is usually done with a hardware device, but for the average application, you may not need a dedicated hardware appliance to serve all your content.

The Web server affords you the opportunity to make changes behind the scenes with minimal impact rather than a dramatic impact. Keep the application server handling the dynamic data, and use the Web server for all static content. The types of files generally served by the Web server are .css, .js, and .html files. There are multiple benefits to doing this, but some detriments as well. The downside is that it will take more time and effort to configure the Web servers, and when pushing content, you will need to push the content separate from the application. The benefit of going with this approach, though, is that you can off-load all the static content onto the Web servers, and keep the application server focused on the dynamic content. Moving your content to a Web server works for a number of situations, but there are always situations where you may have limited impact—and in some cases, negative performance—from using this solution. The bottom line is that you need to test out the application you are deploying, and keep in mind that you will need to tune the Web servers to get the optimal performance.

Routing Algorithms

There are a number of routing algorithms you can use to route traffic. I won't mention all of them, for the simple reason that I haven't had much success with using them. Mainly, because not all application server requests are created equal. The application server is different from a static Web site because the content is dynamically generated and we may need to maintain state in the application. If a server instance goes down, you must have the data on a backup or failover server to handle the request. Another factor is that the application server is serving dynamic data, whereas with Web servers, as long as you get a response from the server you know the end user will get data back. The dynamic requests that are reliant on multiple back-end systems may be responding to the Web requests, while the dynamic requests are failing. If you go with a least-connections approach, what do you think will happen when one of the servers gets a "500" error and is unable to handle requests? Unless you have logic in place to test for the 500 error, the server may be the least busy and get all of the traffic. As a result, all new users will get errors.

Round-Robin

The routing algorithm I most often recommend is round-robin. There may be cases where other algorithms are superior, but my experience is that the round-robin, overall, has been the most effective way to route traffic between a load balancer and the Web servers. I then rely on the proxy server to handle the routing between the Web server and applications server. This gives me the best control over the content I want served from the Web servers and the content that is sent back to the application server. There have been a few cases where the round-robin straight to an application server is superior, such as when you have remote calls to an application server (such as with RMI), or you have few to no images, and the application is more of a business layer.

Server Availability and Application Availability

Application-server failover has a number of subtle distinctions that need to be understood before creating an application-server failover strategy and best-case approach to accomplishing multiple scenarios. The distinction has to do with whether the end user has to retry his client request or the system will handle the failure and can proceed without user interaction. Assume you are in the middle of a transaction. You have data that is in the process of committing, and then there is an exception. If you truly want failover, you would need to either roll back the transaction, or pick up the transaction on the failover server and complete the transaction from there. The subtle distinction is between your wanting the end-user to know about the failure, or you're handling it for the end user.

Server availability is basically whether you have a physical machine or application server that you can fall back on if the application runs into a condition that requires it. If you have two servers, then yes, you have server availability—if Server A fails then you can go to Server B. It is also important to ask if you need to retry the business request or if the system will handle it for you. The end user or client may have to retry his request after getting a system exception. You don't need to worry about the transaction—you only need to have a server available for a retry. The client will be fully aware that an exception occurred and that he will need to resubmit his request before the transaction can go through. Server availability is the easiest way to handle failover and can be done at configuration. When you want to take this to the next level, you want to route to a server that is available to handle the request and also make sure that the Java components in the system are available as well. Designing a system that has server availability is pretty straightforward and can be done at implementation.

Application availability is when you failover to the redundant system. Is the application in a position where you can continue where it left off? That is, if you are filling out form XYZ, and the system goes down, do you end up at a blank page that requires you to start over, or is part of your data there, or is the whole form already filled out for you? (For argument's sake, I assume the persistence will be done at the server level.) Understand that if a common component has failed, and you fail the request over to a server that is connected to the same dependent system, you will have failures at the failover. Even when you design the system to handle failover, you need to be aware of the common components. The more difficult approach is to make the application aware of transactions and the point at which it would need to either commit or roll back.

Cluster Approach

Clustering the application is, for the most part, a configuration task that takes place after the application is built in development and is on its way to production. A developer must follow some rules in order for clustering to work correctly. The most important rule is that objects inside the application must implement serializable; implementing serializable allows your Java objects to be converted to bytes and is critical when using session replication. The reason for this is simple: when the application server is ready to save session data on the backup server, it will serialize the data and send it to the backup server. If the Java classes are not serializable, then that object will not be available on the server you failed over. Any objects that you do not want to have replicated across the clusters need to be marked so that they are not replicated by the container. This includes logging framework components and classes for which you want the only copy on the local instance.

Large versus Small Clusters

I am frequently asked which is the better approach—a large cluster or multiple smaller clusters? This is one of the most common questions, and the real answer is, "It depends." I can lay out the pros and cons of both approaches and let the customer decide what he wants to do. It isn't just a simple task to set up domain-environments scripts and procure the hardware. If you choose to have many small domains, you could have an administrative nightmare that will cost you time and effort. And all it takes is for one downstream application to be unavailable, and the whole system fails, regardless of the configuration. Setting up interdependent systems can be complex; it requires a lot of testing to do it correctly. If you can decouple applications and have a failover plan in place to handle such situations, then do it. But keep the application's core function in mind. Is it worth the cost to have the additional overhead?

Multiple Applications One Cluster

Due to the high cost of capital equipment, the labor involved, and the licensing costs of these systems, a common approach is to put a host of applications on a single cluster. This approach is valid for development environments and non-business critical systems. From a cost perspective, I think that unless the application runs perfectly all the time, there are going to be issues. In a shared environment, you have a single operating system, shared drives, and other shared resources. All these resources must be shared across all the applications. When you put multiple applications on a shared environment, you have to assume all the neighbors will be courteous and respect your privacy. This isn't always the case. Quite frequently, you may have altercations when trying to deploy all these applications together. Application code written for Application A can also have an impact on Application B, if your applications are sharing frameworks that may have shared resources. There are ways inside of the application, however, to separate, at configuration level, the number of threads allocated to each of the applications. I know this works because I have done it. But what if one of the applications needs to be recycled? Then you recycle all of the applications. Make sure that you have put applications that have similar use patterns together, and don't deploy those that are resource intensive and cause outages in the other applications.

Some software domains up the server at the operating system and is available for both UNIX and Windows. In practice, however, I have not found them to be effective. My assumption is that the particular circumstances were poorly configured, and if properly configured, they would perform better. You can't pick your neighbors when you are forced to share resources. Although you may be careful with your code, your neighbor may not be. This leads to intermittent performance problems and in some cases, outages due to what the neighbor did with his applications. Also, when doing performance tuning, I have lost control of some of my key variables. There is always a trade off of cost versus performance in any system. The key is in being able to identify the inherent risks and then get buy off from the business units if these risks are acceptable. And in some cases, these decisions are common sense—take, for example, a stock-trading system that's down for a week versus a time-management system. With the trading system, you will be losing your customer's money and may go out of business. The time-management system is not customer-centric and may not impact the bottom line if it is down.

Decouple Business from Presentation

Decoupling the business layers from presentation has the presentation view and model in separate physical deployments. You may run across applications occasionally that decouple the presentation/view from the model. The client may be an applet or an application developed on Java Web start, or another Web application getting business data. The client invokes that business logic from a remote connection and maintains state on the client. In this situation, you may be maintaining state both at the client and the server. There can be a number of challenges when trying to use this architecture. The client (or fat client) contains some business logic and requires a client JAR to communicate with the back-end. This is a drawback because now you must find a way to have server side jars available on the client, this takes up space and bandwidth when downloading the jars if you have a desktop client. Another drawback is that if you use a service locator and cache the connection to the server, you limit the number of clients that can connect to the server. Even when you decouple your application and put your business logic separate from your presentation, you must take into account the granularity of the call and the network latency you will be introducing.

Globally Distributed Systems

If you have a Web site, you most likely are working with globally distributed systems. If you are using a banner ad from an affiliate program or a payment card-processing gateway, there are always dependencies. These services generally have a predefined service-level agreement, and if anything goes wrong, you can vote with your dollar for a new provider. Sure, there will be some integration involved, but you can move to a new service provider. When you are working inside of a company, and the company is its own provider of services, there isn't the financial liability between the customer and the client. You can work very hard to make the most robust system, but another department may have just put something together. Now your application will be only as available as the least-reliable system—unless, of course, you can code around this. That, however, would take foresight, and in many cases, you'll be lucky to get the project completed on time, let alone have the foresight to see and fix nonexistent issues—at least, nonexistent until you get into the production environment. It is also cost prohibitive to maintain such a large number of systems, and keep data in sync across a large environment. Furthermore, having multiple clusters across the globe would be difficult to do. The basic tenet is that you may not be able to easily distribute the system without certain risk based on what the application's function is.

Business Logic Testing

To successfully know your response times for the application, you can do deterministic testing of your applications to sample transactions in the environment. But you encounter a problem when your sampling happens more frequently than the customer's logging in. You may have a development group, production group, and business unit sampling the environment, too. The additional number of users coming into the system will determine how much overhead you will have to support. The goal is to find one area on which you can focus, and keep your efforts on that one metric. Metrics can be as simple as a script that logs into the servers, calculates response times, and produces a report. If you are interested in drilling down even further, you can use a product that instruments the code with a timer around your business logic. You have to be careful if you instrument every line of code, though, because you are introducing a lot of additional overhead that you may have not designed the system to handle.

Many companies use tools to keep Web metrics on their application performance. The tools usually log in and do some business logic on the servers and check for some verbiage on the page. If the verbiage exists, then they say "Success" and mark the time it took from the log-in screen to finding the data on the screen. The log-ins occur from multiple points of presence throughout the country. The data is stored online and is available through the Web site. Management loves these reports because of the objective nature of the tool, with its clear, concise data that can be customized. Many companies also go a step further and develop tests that periodically log in or do some business logic on the servers. The frequency is higher, and it generally checks the logic on all of the servers. These tests identify individual servers that may be experiencing an issue. These tools are typically homegrown and do not include the added reporting features, but they are good for troubleshooting the servers.

Database Issues

The database is the repository or place to store the critical business and configuration information to run your Web applications. An application written on the first day has a different behavior several months later. The database is a key component and frequently overlooked for those new to Java application servers. When I am called to look at an application's performance, I first ask how the database looks. Most of my experience has been with Oracle, so I will focus on that. When looking at the database, I will always go to a few areas. What are the most used SQL statements? What is the cost associated with each? Getting this report automated and regularly sent to you is imperative during efforts to gain system stability. Ask yourself or the data architect about what can be done to improve performance. Involve the database administrators. Have them monitor the application. Have them check to validate the developers are using prepared statements in your application. Have them occasionally manually flush the shared memory, assuming that it is full. Many database administrators focus on the database structure. They will write in workaround for poor application design when the ownership should be shared and propagated back to the developers.

In every company, batch jobs need to be run for a variety of reasons, from synchronizing users to processing of payment. Keep in mind that when the batch jobs are running, they can lead to a performance situation—the customer may describe the application as slowing down every morning. The slowness is due to some undocumented process that is running against your production database. People need access to production for just about any reason you can imagine, but that doesn't mean they should all be given access. Say that one developer or support person gets access and starts running ad hoc queries. He starts using a few database queries and then moves on to more tools that could cause harm to your systems, like creating tables or exporting the database and accessing it with common spreadsheet software. Weeks or months later, the entire database will lock up due to the unrestricted access to the environments. A friend of mine accidentally brought down an entire production database, just by running a simple query in the database. The first assumption of slowness in the system is that it must be the application server—all issues in the enterprise environment manifest themselves at the application server. You will rarely see an issue with service or a backend component that does not impact the front end in some way.

PRODUCTION

Do You Know What Your Servers Did Last Night?

If you come to work in the morning and don't know exactly what your servers did overnight, there is a problem. From an administrative perspective, you should at least know of any code pushes, server recycles, or server crashes. You should know from the day before if you met your service-level agreements and if not, which components caused you to miss them. The biggest change I went through when starting work on Java application servers was realizing that just because the application server responded to a "ping," that didn't mean the application was working. If you do not know this information, you have not been focusing on monitoring—a key aspect of highly available applications. You should not only monitor the systems, disks, CPUs, and network, but you should also watch the transaction response time and determine which transactions failed. You should have a good understanding of what the customer's experience will be for the day. It is so important to have healthy servers during the night—then, when load starts to peak on Monday morning or at the end of the month, you will be better able to handle the issues.

Tracking what your servers did each night over the course of a week or month will tell you the trends of the system. When you understand the behavior of the system, you can start to trend the application and predict how it will behave today, tomorrow, and next week. For starters, it's okay to focus on just one key metric, the overall transactions per second (TPS). The TPS or the transactions per minute (TPM) shows how many requests your system can handle per unit of time—you can define that as a business transaction or use case. There are tools to instrument your code, or you can put timers in your interfaces to track the business logic. It doesn't matter what metric you key off of, just be consistent with your measurement and trust that you can detect improvement when that metric changes.

Do You Know What Your Employees Did Last Night?

Knowing what your employees did last night indicates how the system is doing. Are they in a reaction mode as they stay up with your servers all night long? Do they come in the next morning, hand over a pager, and go home to bed? Do your developers constantly have their laptops by their sides so they can recompile the code and deploy to production at a moment's notice? There are exceptions to any of these scenarios, but they should not be the norm. Having your employees around to baby-sit an application isn't the best use of their time. If they are so engrossed in recycling applications to fix issues, they aren't learning anything, and the application isn't going to get any better. I've heard managers say, "Well, that's their job. They're here to keep the systems running." I suppose that's right—it *is* their job to keep the systems running. But if you have constant instability, that isn't any way to live. I've had to live with unstable systems that require constant supervision and all of my time and attention. There are also issues with organizational culture; those who dislike the culture can choose to go to a culture that isn't as chaotic as yours. It is a clear failure of management when necessary steps are not taken to bring the systems into a stability mode rather than a reactive mode.

Four 9s Is Difficult

The goal of any business application is getting the application to a production state and production quality. When your manager is asking for 9999 availability (less than 9 hours of downtime a year), you know there is a challenge. From a senior-management perspective, the goal is to keep the applications in budget and ultimately, to keep the customer's business. I am amazed by the number of applications that make it to production unprepared. Consider the amount of downtime you must have to be 100 percent available, and then think about how this compares to your company. Are you 100 percent available? This means that you deployed your application, and it has been available for the whole year without a minute of downtime. Think about the implications of what a truly available application is. Lengths of implementations vary, but consider the amount of time spent every week on installing system patches, updating code, and unexpected outages. If you add all of these outages, I suspect that the typical business application would not even be in the top five slots for availability. My point is this: if your goal is 100 percent availability, this should be factored into the design before you start the development and planning of systems.

If you have experience with deployment or the production environment you know that it isn't unusual to have code pushes and downtime of the systems. You may have an hour here or there but it all adds up. The chart below shows the number of hours of downtime and the percent of availability. Many enterprise applications schedule a couple hour windows a week for downtime and code pushes for application. The time can quickly add up, two hours a week is 104 hours of downtime. Just with the scheduled outages you will have only 98 percent availability, add some unplanned outages to the system and you will have a tough time if not impossible time hitting 99 percent availability.

100% Available
99.9% less than 9 hr/yr
99.5% less than 43 hr/yr
99.0% less than 87 hr/yr
98.0% less than 175 hr/yr

Ex Post Facto (After the Fact)

How do you know when you are successful? You know by looking at situations after the fact, or ex post facto. You look at the facts after the event has happened and can gauge your level of success. When I consult on a system, the manager may ask how it is doing on the next day. I respond, "How do you normally do on a Tuesday at two o'clock in the afternoon on the third week in March?" After giving me a few strange looks, the manager finally arrives at what I need to accurately make an assessment. Business trends shift constantly, and so must the strategy to manage your application systems. The only way to know for sure how you are doing is to audit what you have done; this happens every quarter with a company's performance reports. For example, it expected eight cents a share but got six. You should be able to do this same thing with your systems. Building the data trends and capturing the ex post facto information allows you to trend your application performance. Now that you know what the system has accomplished in the past during peak times, you can predict what the system is going to do under similar circumstances.

You can never truly predict failure, but you can mitigate those failures by putting in stopgap measures to keep servers healthy while you are fixing other issues. If you have ever supported an enterprise application that serves a global market, you understand the issues that you may encounter during the off time. For some, the off time is during the day, for other sites, the middle of the day. It really depends on your target market and your customers' requirements. By knowing what your servers are doing at all times, you ensure continual service with the least amount of downtime. If you don't have a good monitoring system in place, it is time to consider it.

Ad Hoc Changes

I am routinely called by companies that say, "We don't care how long it takes or what you have to do in production to get this application stable." They are in a position where those who take risks play an important role. They have been making changes in production and feel perfectly confident doing so. In a typical company, the best practice is to have all changes go through a change control. These changes must be documented and updated in a document repository, but remember to be practical. With any application, there may come a point when you are going to have downtime and potentially lose millions of dollars over the process. In some cases, the primary goal is to get the application fixed, and let the process folks document until they are satisfied. You should know the implications of the change you are going to make without having to guess if it will make a difference. If you do not have any idea of the changes, then I do not recommend making the changes in a production environment. A consultant for the vendor will be the best resource for you.

Apply similar fixes until you can address the issue. If you have a system that is consuming memory and showing out of memory errors in the log file and you increase threads, you are eventually going to crash the servers. On the other hand, if you understand this information, you can take the right action. (You should decrease the threads and look for areas that can reduce the memory overhead.) Determine what your session time-outs are set to. If EJB, what are your deployment descriptors instructing the code to do? Making ad-hoc changes in production is dangerous, and unless you know the cause and effect of making the change and the expected result, it's best to limit the number of ad-hoc changes.

Root Cause

Never assume that you know what the issue is, and don't just recycle as a periodic fix for your issues. There is always a root cause for an outage or issue, and you must always insist on getting to the root cause of an issue. These issues always have a reason for happening—don't think that the issue is a one-time event. Consider the source when root cause is provided. If there is any doubt in the root cause assessment, press the issue and make sure you have the right root cause. If you fail at this step, you will never be able to get the systems under control. The cycle will continue until there is an accurate diagnosis of the root cause and action steps are taken to prevent it from happening again.

Monitoring

Monitoring is one of the givens in the production environment; there are monitors to cover just about every aspect of the system, from room temperature to systems availability to the application availability. A successful monitoring strategy does not just focus on the services or processes running; it also looks at the business monitoring. It is not good enough to have the servers up and running; the work must be done as well. The main reason for this is that you can have positive results from all of the basic monitors and still have an application that is not working.

I was working on a project to develop some simple business-application monitoring tools that I thought might help the client troubleshoot some of his issues. The goal was to monitor all of the business components, not just the threads and memory utilization. A couple of weeks before the deployment, I asked where we were on the Web application to monitor the system.

"We aren't going to need it," the manager told me—he had, decided to go with his monitoring system that he had used on other non-Java projects.

"Do you realize that we won't get all of the information with just that monitoring?" I asked.

"Oh, I've talked to the lead," he said, "and I'm monitoring several other applications. The lead assured me that value could be provided to the site availability metrics."

In this large enterprise, the lead who was pushing for the monitoring solution was less concerned that if another solution better met the company's needs, then his position would not be needed. He assured the team that he would be able to meet their needs. The manager was sold on the idea of there being a way to do all the monitoring. I respected the manager's decision and didn't create the application.

I asked the monitoring team for reference applications. "This application is part of a sixty-four-instance cluster," I told them. "Are you currently monitoring any applications of that size?"

"No," one team member admitted, "we don't have any of that size."

"Are you monitoring any WebLogic applications?" I then asked.

"We're not—but we do have the tools."

Eventually, the manager came back after the system was in place. "The customers are complaining that the systems are down," he said, "but we have no way to know. The monitoring data tells us that the system is up and running, but the application servers are not."

I didn't say "I told you so," but I could have—the manager went with what he was familiar with because of his networking background. But the issue was that he was working in a new paradigm, one that required him to understand the component availability in the application, rather than whether or not a process was running.

Determine Who Has Access to Production

I once sat with a production support engineer to try to understand what he had been working on so that I could help with the performance issue he was having with the application. The engineer was told that the system had been slow for the past hour. His job was to investigate. I wondered what the problem could be, so I started to ask questions. He pulled up a telnet window, logged into the box, and identified an Emacs (a UNIX-based editor) session that was taking 80 percent of the CPU. He killed the session and tested the application. It now ran much faster.

"How did you know that was the problem?" I asked.

"The developers had access to that box," he explained, "and they were using Emacs to go through the logs."

When the Emacs editors consumed too many resources, the system slowed down. Consequently, the session had to be killed. I asked myself why the developers were in production. Why were there so many logs that they needed to go through them with an editor? I asked why a developer had access to the production system.

The engineer said that the developers had access since they went into production six months ago.

"Has the same thing been happening for the past six months?"

"Yes," he responded.

"Have you told the developers what the Emacs sessions are doing to production?"

He shook his head. "No. And they have permission to be in the system."

This attitude toward the incident completely dumbfounded me. Did he not realize that such a practice was not in the company's best interest? He didn't need to continue to provide access to a person just because he had access to a system resource. And I wondered why he'd waited until a customer experienced the issue and opened up a case before he got this working.

What was this engineer thinking? Why would he dismiss a chance to fix an issue before it became a larger issue? I don't have those answers, but if you get only one thing from this chapter, I hope you realize that in a large, complex system, with so many dependencies, anything could be the reason for performance issues. The system is a relatively fragile ecosystem that requires maintenance care and most importantly vigilance.

That engineer should have initially gone to the developer and asked if he really needed access to the logs. He could have offered to move them over to a development box. Then a batch job or other utility monitoring should have been used to monitor for high CPU processes. Understanding the whole system requires knowing more than just the environment. Talk to those people you are supporting and working with; you can learn a lot from reading about things in a book or experiencing it firsthand, but you can also learn a great deal from other people. Think about the production issues you see on a daily basis—how many of these could be fixed by empowering the employees to come forward with ideas on how to increase performance, just by making a process change?

Unauthorized Access

Having the most robust code in place with the best database design doesn't make any difference if you have unauthorized users accessing key systems. Companies sometimes allow users access to the production systems. There are a number of reasons for this, but a big factor is the time-to-market of these systems, or there isn't enough time to build the supporting structures for the system to work. The IT department may have said they just don't have the cycles to finish the reporting needed by the business, so as an exception, they let one person into the database to run a report. That report turned into two reports, then three, then the report was run daily or hourly. Another analyst asked for the user name and password, and before they knew it, there were multiple people running reports against the production systems.

There should always be a limit on when and how often nonproduction support folks have access to these systems. Production support may not have a clue of why the systems are crashing, but the answer lies at some marketing analyst's desk who found a way to access the production system. He hooked up a query tool and is exporting all the data in the database. There are ways to mitigate this risk, but from a security perspective, why risk your online system without having the governance systems in place to thwart an internal attack from another department?

Here's an example: I had to deal with a customer who had over forty million customers, and of those customers, about twenty thousand logged in at any one time. A database provided content to one of the online shopping carts, and the system would come to a crashing halt without any warning. After investigating multiple log files and various systems, the main culprit turned out to be a developer, who happened to have access to the production system and was testing to see if content was available for a production deployment. One developer with access to the database was able to bring down the entire system with just one command. I have seen this happen at other companies, too—businesses use query tools to check statistics on sales inventory use. Even though most of these accounts are read-only, you can easily tie up a database, which leads to an entire system shutdown. As for the user who needs the data, he can't do his job without access, and the production folks don't have the bandwidth or resources to support this effort. There are ways you can govern access to the system and make both parties come to an amicable agreement on who should have access and when. Within reason, the only person or entity that should have access to the online production system is the application itself. Computers and large storage devices are becoming cheaper and cheaper. It doesn't take that much effort to replicate the database on another server. If you do have a lot of data, then it is time to consider implementing a data-mart strategy to allow marketing access to critical data—they need to make decisions.

Controlled Chaos

If you subscribe to the chaos theory, you know that an entire application is the sum of its components. If you want to know how a large cluster of sixty servers is going to perform, it is very simple. If you study the behavior of one server, you know that if you multiply those issues by sixty, you will get a pretty good idea of how the large cluster will behave. There are other factors that come into play, but, for the most part, this holds true. This is one of the keys to success when it comes to the technical design of the application server. When one of the sixty servers has a property file that is wrong, you have a one in sixty chance of hitting it. For each of the variables that are wrong on the server, you increase your likelihood of hitting one of these issues. This is why it is so important to modularize repetitive aspects of your system and automate when possible.

Multi-Homing Your Application

To conserve on resources, companies are deploying multiple applications to shared environments. This ranges from a few applications to tens of applications. Let's say you have two development teams that developed applications separate from each other. Team A was very cautious. They took care of their code and were very careful when allocating objects. This was not true of Team B. Their application was constantly crashing and causing the servers to go down. When you deploy the applications together, remember that they are sharing the same space; one will impact the other. You may save money by deploying them together, but you risk losing business in the near term, as well as your reputation. If you improperly deploy an application or don't consider what it is doing, you can very easily create outages with all of your applications, instead of the one that is most affected. Separate the applications in the interim, and develop a work-around to keep services at the required service-level agreement. Once you have them safely apart, form a special team to find and resolve the issues. Sitting in a room with other engineers to resolve system issues is difficult and time consuming, but sometimes this is the only way to come to a resolution. I often wonder why engineers would shy away from coming together and working through the issues. I see it as a win-win for all involved—you stand to learn a lot from the discussions and understand how the application fits together.

Once you get the issues under control, you can go about your daily work. Management should be aware of your efforts to make the environment better. If you don't have their approval, build a case to get some time to focus on the issues. The big issues usually get a lot of attention, but it all depends on how you go about looking at it.

Log Level for Production

An age-old debate occurs when a developer and production support meet on logging. The support engineers demand to know why an application is performing poorly. The developer says an answer cannot be given until he sees the debug log files. The problem is that one of the reasons the application is performing so poorly is due to the debug logging. So how do we compromise so both developer and support get what they need? I think there needs to be compromise on how to reach a level where both parties are able to get their needs met without compromising the stability of the application. There is no reason to have full debug turned on in a production environment. The debug logging is a tool used to help the developer understand, at a very fine-grained level, what the application is doing through each step. This is normally down to the method level, is extremely verbose, and will fill hundreds of megabytes of log files in a matter of minutes. But it is not enough to say that you are going to turn off logging; you also need to check before you create that object if debug is enabled, regardless of whether you want to log it. There can be additional overhead on the logging framework to create these objects in memory, even though they were not written to disk. In order for that logger to print the message to a disk, he must first convert it to a string, and then get hold of a synchronized resource, such as a buffered log writer.

I was brought on-site to troubleshoot some performance issues at a customer site. I took a look at what the threads had been doing by doing a thread dump, and I started looking at the stack traces in the log file. I found that the performance bottleneck was due to the amount of logging the customer had enabled. There were six places in the code where it was waiting to get hold of the log file to write the debug statement to it. All the debug statements went to one of the configured server logs. What this meant was that the logging was now adding time onto the total amount of time it took to log the message. The thread of execution or execute thread is going to have to wait for resources from the virtual machine to be able to log that message.

The synchronization block inside of the logger is a line in which each thread must wait before finishing the work. If logging is a requirement, consider this up front in the business requirements so you can adequately plan for it. Consider, though, that too much debug can cause OutOfMemory errors and make the server crash. The conversion of debug statements to a String (an immutable object); even if you do not write the object to disk, you have still created an object that must be garbage collected. I have personally been a part of load tests, where the load tests were under the identical load, the only difference being the level of debug. The load test with debug turned on caused an OutOfMemory error, while the one with debug turned off never once ran into a memory issue.

Monitoring

Monitoring is one of those areas that is so important to the stability of the applications of the production applications. The challenge with monitoring is that with so many tools and ways to monitor, how do you know where to start? I like to break down the application into six areas for monitoring. The complexity and customization increases as you go down the list at the final level. At "Business Level Monitoring" you will write custom code to monitor your business-level activities.

Network & Infrastructure Monitoring: Using common monitoring programs you can monitor the operating-systems network utilization and disk availability.

Services Monitoring: Monitors the services you need to run the application and can be processes or Windows services.

Application Level Component Monitoring: Moving higher up the stack, the application-level monitoring is within the applications you have running. Are there components that need to be running in order for your applications to work?

Deterministic Testing: There may be issues in the application where you need to have certain functionality working. Let's say you have a com call or http call that you can emulate in code. The deterministic testing is used to test to see if pieces of the application are working.

Business-Level Monitoring: Business-level monitoring is where you identify several synthetic transactions that you can initiate to test business functionality in the application.

Transactional Monitoring: Transactional monitoring is the ability to look at every transaction that is required to complete a business process. The goal is to know if you started a transaction and whether that transaction ended.

The tools you use don't always have to be Java-based or expensive monitoring suites. Many successful scripts are written in whatever the team is comfortable supporting. These monitoring efforts are ongoing. Start monitoring a few key areas, and if you need to add more, you can do so later. Be careful when trying to monitor everything—this will only frustrate those who are inundated with pages and alerts for the system.

Large Cluster Monitoring

There really isn't one ideal way to monitor a large cluster of application servers. There are many methods, and no one method is better than any other. The most successful examples of large clusters have a combination of off-the-shelf packages and scripts and monitoring tools. Be careful not to purchase any tools before you understand what the key metrics you need from the system, and what components you will need to monitor to get that data. When going into large companies to look into their monitoring tools, you will inevitably find monitoring suites sitting on the shelves or being completely underutilized. Knowing what to monitor and when to take action reduces the average time to repair. If you know exactly what will break and when, you will know when to fix the problem before it arises. In an *n*-tier environment, as the number of systems increases, so does the risk of having a system failure due to a poorly designed application or an improperly configured database. You should start monitoring availability on the downstream systems. This may be contrary to what you would normally think to monitor first: your own application. For the most part, the front end applications are reliant on the data from a database or other repository, but most of that dynamic data comes from or goes into a downstream system.

It is extremely important to develop the right solution, one that meets the business needs, especially when dealing with third-party vendors or existing enterprise systems. When a system depends on a downstream system, any delay in data may lead to a system outage on front-end application. The downstream impact is a system-wide outage—a chain is only as strong as the weakest link. The best way to mitigate these issues is to expect failure at every level. In the enterprise, you may have control over your domain, but you may be unable to control other domains. A dependency on your landing page on a downstream application will make your application as stable as the downstream system. If you combine this with multiple downstream systems, your application is only as available as the sum of the downstream systems. A good plan will document and well define all failures in a system. Once you have the failure points identified, test to see how your application behaves when one of those systems goes down.

In an enterprise, I sometimes like to monitor the downstream systems more than the front-end systems. By looking at the systems I depend on, I take the first step to quickly identify issues. You, too, will start to understand the dependency implications. When building a high-availability system, understand the end-user's perception when a system goes down. For example, consider what happens when a user logs into an application. He might not be able to do any other work, but if he can log in to the application, the focus shifts to the application or functionality he is trying to access within the Web application and not the application itself. Understanding the technical architecture is just as important as understanding the application design. Determine which services are being monitored and the frequency of monitoring. When monitoring a system, it is important to know when the system goes down and to have a log of the system instabilities. You will quickly tie the issues faced in the application to a downstream component; knowing the failure pattern will help build certain patterns to watch for. System availability you can monitor at the page level, method level, database level, or the dependent services. Monitoring the application from the bottom up is a step in building your high-performance system. As you monitor, you will understand the overall response times and page-load times—a business is usually interested in these metrics. Initially, your instinct may be to hide the results from the business if there is poor performance of the Web site. But now that you have a way to test, you can make changes and will have an idea when your changes are making a difference. The page-load times will be spelled out right in front of you. If you don't like the results, the alternative is to fix the issues that prevent you from achieving those goals.

Centralized Administration

As your server clusters grow, or as you maintain a large number of applications across various environments, the need to be organized and have tools in place becomes increasingly important. Managing a single server can be challenging by itself, but when you add the additional overhead of handling multiple systems, the job becomes more challenging. This is an excellent example of where automation can give you economies of scale when building, deploying, and managing systems.

All the administrators go to the centralized administration when they want to know about a domain. The central administration provides a single repository for all the administrative needs of the application domain. You can manage your builds, deployments, and server-management scripts from this location. Make sure you back up this server; you may even want to have a cold standby server available to take over in case the server goes down.

Whenever you go to a central administration model, you limit the number of places you need to go for changes. At the same time, one mistake on the administration server will affect all other servers in the same way. Define a strategy to implement and test your new central model, and distinguish the difference between a successful backup plan and a poor one. Because you never know when a system component is going to fail, test both servers equally, and make sure they are included in the normal backup plan. When I build an application management strategy, I find it most helpful to build the process as I work through the issues in the environment. Getting the administration system in place is going to take time and multiple iterations before it will work as expected, and should be included in the quality assurance life cycle. The larger the environment the better the economies of scale. If you are working in a smaller application, building all of these automation processes may be overkill, but it is great practice when it comes time to work with larger farms.

TROUBLESHOOTING THE ISSUES

Troubleshooting 101

Not everyone is good at troubleshooting. That may be because "troubleshooting" is more than being able to troubleshoot issues at the root of the problem; it also involves having problem-solving skills. Getting good at troubleshooting takes practice, and many people never get the chance to test their skills in production environments. Troubleshooting requires common knowledge of networking, development, databases, and Web servers. But once you have the common knowledge, you must also be a good problem solver—with a healthy appetite for a challenge. You also need the ability to deal with intense periods of focus, while regulating the amount of time you spend in a certain direction before moving on. Many times, a good problem solver only needs a few key pieces of data to narrow down the issue. On the other hand, the number of issues you encounter may be endless. I have seen issues with network latency, bugs in the virtual machine, environmental issues, Web servers, load balancers—the list goes on. Of the many issues, you just don't know which one is causing the problem.

Where to Start Looking for Trouble

How do I know where to start looking for trouble? I remember the old saying: When you look for trouble, you usually will find it. Knowing where to start can be somewhat scientific, but mostly, you'll learn where to start by experiencing the issues. The more you work through issues, the more your intuition kicks in—at some point, you will develop almost a sixth sense about applications. The first thing to do is talk to someone who is very familiar with the system and the issues at hand. This person is usually very technical and relays what he sees as the core problem. From a technology perspective, the highest-ranked issues—those that impact the most people—are always considered first. You will find that many engineers do not focus on issues that could be simple fixes and improve the user's experience. For example, consider a server that occasionally slows down. Most administrators will wait until a trouble ticket is opened concerning the slow-down. Then the administrator will look at the server and admit that it is slow; they will recycle the server and move on. From business continuity, this practice is a warning signal the company is in reactive mode. Don't wait until the end user's experience is bad before doing something about the issue. From a trouble-shooting perspective, take some core metrics periodically on the server's health. Metrics give you indicators as to when you may run into problems.

Rule #1: Issues do not resolve themselves. There is a reason for every issue, and if the issue isn't fixed, it mostly likely will occur again.

Rule #2: Never assume that someone else will fix the problem. If you don't take an active role in finding issues and getting them fixed, they will not get solved.

Rule #3: The more time you spend complaining about the situation, the less time you will have to find the solution.

Rule #4: If you don't think the problem is yours, think again. Regardless of whether you are a project manager or manager, it is your job to help with the resolution.

Ask the Right Questions

The first question always should be, "Has this ever worked in the environment?" If the answer is yes, the next question is, "What changed between the time it was working and when it stopped working?" If the application never worked, then you will need to start by identifying all the log files and drilling down into what the issue is. In some cases, it won't be a cut-and-dry issue, so you will need to look beyond just the application logs you have. Vendors put debug flags in their code that may give you more insight into what the application is doing, but be careful—too much information in a log will overwhelm your ability to narrow down on an issue. Changes can happen in any number of dependent systems, so be careful not to rule out things like network upgrades, operating system patches, and scheduled changes. Although it's important to look out for issues that are caused by the environment, it's just as important to know when to have a healthy skepticism. Even though there was a change, it may not be the reason for the issue. Understanding the environment and getting a deeper knowledge of Java application servers and *n*-tier systems will help you determine this.

Memory or Threads

When I first approach a system that is behaving poorly, I first look at two indicators: memory (of the virtual machine) and threads (execution threads). If it is a situation where all the threads are doing work, and the application is slow, then I know to look at the threads for an indication of why the server is having issues. I can determine if it is a thread issue by taking a thread dump of the virtual machine in question. It's a good idea to write a script that will take thread dumps for analysis later. This collection of data will help you better determine why the issue occurred, and once you have the root cause identified, you can build and predict the behavior of your applications.

Differences between Environments

If your application will be deployed on a cluster in production, you should be clustering in development. This point is so important, yet I frequently encounter situations where this is ignored. Business applications are written to be deployed into production, yet the environments may not look like the environment into which they are going to deploy them. And not only should they have the cluster configured in the development environment, but the patch levels and operating system should be the same as well. Any difference in an environment can be a potential reason for failure in the system later. Knowing how each environment is configured and what patches are in it will decrease the time to issue resolution—time won't be wasted in learning about the application server that will be used in production; developers will use the ones they are familiar with.

Consider this example: A developer writes the code in an open-source container and then deploys on a commercially available version. If the developer did not test the code on the application server to which he is deploying, the application will not work. This causes an issue, which will then take additional work and time to get the environments up and running. This is all about taking responsibility for your code. If you aren't thinking about these issues now, you will when you're called early in the morning.

Load Balancer

The load balancer balances the traffic between multiple Java application servers or Web servers. My experience has been that load balancers work great when each request has equal weight; that is, each request basically consumes the same amount of resources. The challenge with an application server may be that Request A is for a simple Web page, and Request B involves complex business logic. Now, using a straightforward routing logic could evenly distribute load, but the requests are of unequal weight. Meaning that one request takes more resources than the other.

Like any component, the load balancer needs to be tested in the entire environment, just like the rest of the application components. You most likely will run into issues when you get into the production realm if you try to do all you're testing directly hitting the Java application server and not use a load balancer. The load balancers are not extremely complex, but there are settings and configuration options for things like how you do your load balancing, whether you are using sticky or not, or what the load-balancing algorithm is, even if the load balancers you currently use in production have the capacity to handle your new applications. You must test these options before going to production.

Java Virtual Machine

The Java Virtual Machine, or JVM, is software that runs and interprets byte code or object code, rather than letting hardware run the byte code. The JVM, which is operating-system dependent, is available on many operating systems. The theory with interpreted languages is that you only need to write your application once before you deploy on any system. In reality, you will need to consider some operating-system dependencies.

It is a misconception that all JVMs are created equal; they are all based on the specification but may differ, based on the vendor, and they may choose different memory management or handling of shared memory. For example, the JVM settings are just as important as the code you write. Each vendor has his own set of configuration parameters, and his implementation may be a little different from the next one. There is a tight coupling between the application server version you are using and the Java virtual machine. So you will need to check with the version of the application server you are installing, and make sure that you are running with a supported virtual machine. Some Java application servers ship with a compatible version of the virtual machine. Make sure that you are running your application server with the right version of the virtual machine. The most frequent change to the virtual machine is in configuring more memory. The trend with applications is that their footprint gets larger and larger as the applications become more feature-rich. To solve some of the issues, you occasionally will need to dive down to understand how the Java virtual machine (JVM) was implemented.

I have run into several issues where I had to get the JVM vendor involved to fix core virtual-machine bugs. When you choose your application server and virtual machine, make sure you also consider the operating system it will be running on. A customer may be going to production on UNIX, but in the interest of time and/or money, he wants to load test on a Windows operating system. If you aren't load testing on the same server hardware with which you are going to production, it is almost pointless to be testing at all. You certainly may be able to identify the methods that are performing poorly, but that is only a small part of the application. When building your system, consider application servers, virtual machines, developers, and code.

Threads

Threads allow applications to simultaneously do work, with-out threads applications are serial in their ability to process work requests—this means you need to complete one task before moving on to the next. The second unit of work can't start until the first unit of work is finished. Threads are extremely important to providing an application that scales and handles large volumes of work. There is also a relationship between the number of threads you have and the system CPUs. The more CPUs on the box, the more threads you will be able to handle and as a result, the more work you can do. There is a trade-off between the number of threads allocated and the CPU utilization. Virtual threads or threads map to an abstraction layer in the Java virtual machine, which map to a CPU thread. Each CPU can only have one unit of work occurring simultaneously. I believe there is a change with how the dual core technology, where the CPU can handle multiple requests at once. The theory is the same, though; the abstraction layer has multiple threads that all compete for the limited number of CPU resources. The more threads you give to an application, the more simultaneous requests you can send through to the CPU. Give it too much work, and there will be more contexts switching at the CPU. This additional context switching will slow down the performance of your CPU and ultimately result in poor application performance.

Context Switching

Too much context switching is bad; when tuning a system, you must be aware of the consequences of making changes to the application server. This translates to the architecture and design of the system as well. Here's a common misconception: if we have a system that is poorly performing, we will just throw more resources at it. Well, that doesn't always work; in fact, you can cause more harm than good. At some point, you will get diminishing returns by adding more threads to a system. The only option is to add more server instances of the application. The architecture may need to be adjusted, depending on how many virtual machines you plan to run on a server.

Operating Systems

A number of the projects on which I've worked did not spend as much time designing and choosing the operating system and disk configuration as they did choosing the coffee for the break room. The operating system you choose directly impacts the amount of time you will spend troubleshooting and deploying your application. I have worked with the various types of operating systems, and I realize that there are benefits to working with Windows as well as with UNIX-based systems. When choosing your operating system, unless you are deploying on the exact same hardware, you may run into system-related issues, just by developing on Windows and deploying on UNIX.

I ran into a situation where the application worked fine on Windows, but when it was deployed on Linux, the application didn't work. The problem was that the base encoding for Windows was different from Linux, and it took a few hours to figure that out. The more complicated the application, the more components there are, and you can impact timelines by not testing on the right operating system.

It is always a good idea to develop an understanding of the requirements and try to foresee the issues you may have. If you can predict the problems before they happen, then you can avoid the issue altogether. Also, if you go from Windows to UNIX, realize that your script may not easily migrate to the UNIX platform. You most likely will need to do a complete rewrite of the supporting scripts.

Java Code

The code you write for your application is as important as any other components. You should have an understating of the code in which the Java application servers are written. This is also the programming language you will use to write and customize your business applications. Having a fundamental understanding of Java code will give you an advantage over those who do not understand Java—even over those who understand other programming languages. The best advice I can give you regarding the code is to take the simplest approach to solving problems. You can do a lot of things with the code, but as the main goal is to solve a business objective, keep your code straightforward, and document well and often. If you are faced with a requirement that seems as if you need to write a lot of custom code, be cautious. Unless your code is amazing because it solves something that no one else knows how to do, just keep your code simple. The more standards you use in your code, the easier it will be to transition support and troubleshoot.

Disks

The choice of hard drives, the raid level, and which parts of the applications you install on which disk has a significant impact on the application's performance. The most common requirement I see has to do with the size of the disks. In an enterprise, all this storage goes on the storage area network (SAN) for all of the disk needs. A properly configured SAN can have super performance, but it adds another level of complexity. If possible, I like to see the application deployed locally, rather than on a SAN.

Threads

From a design and project management perspective, there should be a way to aggregate all of the results so that you understand the relationship between the increasing number of threads and the application. It isn't just from the thread perspective; it's from the interdependencies by increasing threads. If I increase threads, I am giving an okay to the application to consume more resources. The CPU is also given the signal to increase context switching. When you determine that you have a thread-contention issue and zero idle threads to service the next incoming request, take a thread dump from the servers. Thread dumps taken approximately every fifteen seconds will tell you if the application is blocking. If it is blocking, it will show what the application is locking on. You will want to look for the thread that seems to be doing similar activities, but only one of the threads is farther into an object than the others. The thread dump is an absolute must when troubleshooting Java application servers. At first, a thread dump may seem complex and may not make a lot of sense, but over time and with enough practice, the process becomes less difficult. And the wealth of information you get from looking at thread dumps is valuable. It gives you the ability to narrow down to the line of code where the problems are.

When you see all the threads consumed, this usually means trouble. Check for objects that are locked, and try to determine what is trying to gain access to this resource. Thread dumps can be very confusing, and looking at them for the first time can be intimidating. Try using a tool to analyze the thread dumps for you. One of the more helpful tools I have used is the Samurai thread analyzer. The tool gives you a quick, graphical view to the threads in your application, and it gives you the ability to quickly know if there is an issue. Understanding how to analyzing thread dumps can be quite detailed, but all you really need to know is that a thread dump is one of the most important pieces of information you can get from an application server when troubleshooting issues. Once you master how to analyze thread dumps, you will be ready to solve more complex issues. The more you solve, the better you will get at it.

The second key piece of data to collect is the verbose garbage collection. This data is extremely important in determining applications memory consumption. The verbose garbage collection data shows how much memory is being used by the system and can lead you to potential memory problems in your application. The number of garbage collections can indicate if an application is improperly tuned. It may indicate that several objects are being created and destroyed. Using this information, you can also infer a lot of other things about the application server. You can tune the session's timeout parameter with this, and you can get an idea of the size of session by looking at the overall heap size versus the number of active sessions on the box. The servers are a delicate balance of the right code with the right settings. It isn't always something you can figure out the first time you see the issue, but you will eventually understand and build a high-performance application.

Search Engines

The largest wealth of information is going to come from searching the Internet for the exception or issues you see in your application. Knowing what to search on is almost as much of an art as science when finding the solutions to your problems. Use the search engines when you have identified a behavior that you can't explain or when you see a stack trace that you haven't seen before. When searching the Internet, take care not to immediately associate the stack trace you find with the solutions you find on the Web. Read the stack trace very carefully, and make sure the stack traces line up closely. It can take some time before you can recognize good exceptions from bad ones. If you never do any searches, you most likely won't learn the difference. I used to follow a process of elimination when trying to determine what was wrong. After making it past step 1, I moved onto step 2, and kept going until I ran out of steps. If I stopped making forward progress on the issue, then I would start asking others for help to find a path of escalation.

Involve the Vendors

I have worked on some fascinating, challenging issues that were very deceptive when I first looked at them. One of them appeared to be a memory leak in the application, but it turned out that the Java virtual machine or database driver had the leak. Until you drill down into your application, it is hard to know what changes you should make. For example, I worked on one issue where an IBM virtual machine was running on a WebLogic server. I was completely lost on how to solve the issue. The normal telltale sign was pointing me in the wrong direction. I took my thread dumps and said that the server was not doing anything special; it just got to a point where it completely slowed down. At one moment, the server's queue shot up to thousands until the server finally needed to be killed and restarted. After analyzing the thread dump, the threads appeared normal. The verbose memory output showed there was at least 128 megabytes of virtual RAM left. I finally sent the logs to the vendor to get an idea of what was happening.

After placing a follow-up call to the vendor, the support representative quickly said it was a fragmentation issue. I had quite a bit of experience with this, but I wondered why I hadn't known. After several conference calls, I found out that it was a known issue. The virtual machine assumed that the developer had written optional code. I found out that the virtual machine, over the course of running, would finally reach a point when it could not allocate a contiguous space for its memory. For example, let's say the application needed 25 megabytes of memory to perform an operation. The virtual machine had 138 megabytes available but scattered throughout the virtual machine and not in one contiguous block to allocate. Because it technically was not out of memory, a memory error was never thrown. The lesson here is that if something doesn't fit the paradigm, and it seems to be a little off, involve the vendor. He may have run into this issue before.

Escalate

Escalation in a timely fashion helps everyone. Not everyone can solve every problem. When it comes to business continuity, carefully weigh the cost and benefit associated with the escalation of issues you are not able to solve or the issues the front line support is not able to take care of for you. This does not indicate that the people working on the application have failed, and it usually does not indicate that they are unqualified or unable to handle the job. It is simply about business and doing what is necessary to have business continuity.

I have seen a lot of issues and worked with hundreds of support engineers when dealing with support organizations. To the customer, it appears that support only has to work on his case. In reality, of course, support may be working on ten cases at the same time. Obviously, 100 percent effort can't be given to ten cases simultaneously. The engineers need to prioritize their time and make the best decisions possible, while recognizing that there is always room for error. When escalating to someone's backline manager, talk to the engineer first and ask his opinion. Ask something like, "Are you working on other cases, or are you at a stopping point with this issue?" And ask if this issue could be solved faster if, as a customer, you escalated on your side. Let the engineer make the decision and keep him in the loop. Thank him for working on the issue. You will want to keep a good relationship with him, as well as with everyone with whom you work.

The War Room

The war room, or situation room, is where everyone goes to focus on a particular issue or task. The war room is a great place to be a hero and get noticed, but if you make a mistake, it can have an adverse affect. You will not find a better place, however, to come together as a team to get things resolved. First and foremost, get management's approval before secluding yourself for a week in the war room. And while you're there, don't barricade your team in, and keep everyone else out. (It also does not work well if you are the only person in the room.)

You will need whiteboards, large Post-it notes, Internet access, a phone—and several treats. If you have all of the right people in the room, then things can get moving pretty fast toward resolution. If you don't, then you might as well go back to your desk and accept defeat; the application will continue to get worse.

Personally, I don't like to sit idle in the room. The war room should be filled with activities, including multiple efforts and project teams working on specific areas. It should also be moving quickly toward a resolution by keeping issues confined to the task at hand. I have been in some war room conferences that lasted twenty-four hours a day—shifts came in. I have seen people throw down their pagers and walk out. You may make some friends, but those you thought were friends may become bitter enemies. It is always someone else's fault that you are in the room. You will quickly discover that not all people are up to the challenge of working though issues. You will find several different types of people in the war room. Imagine a room with twenty to thirty people gathered around one conference room table. You can quickly pick out the different type of people:

Type 1: This person usually brings a movie. The movie starts out on someone's laptop, but once he gets a chance at the projector, the movie is in wide screen format and the whole room will be distracted.

Type 2: This person does his normal daily work just like any other day at the office. He writes e-mails, updates spreadsheets, and just does his usual work. He might be doing personal work, including checking e-mail or writing family and friends.

Type 3: This person generally surfs the Internet and does everything except what is related to work. He is extremely easy to pick out. He will send you an occasional funny e-mail or interesting Web site. He uses instant messaging and sometimes just listens through headphones.

Type 4: This person actively investigates and works the issue. He takes sample writing code. If he is not very technical, he will try to get a layperson's understanding of what is happening.

With all the various types of people that you can have in a war room none is more important than the other. The resolution to the issues can come from anyone. Knowing you have multiple personalities does require good leadership to facilitate the issues and lead to a quick resolution, but that doesn't mean that someone who is a manager or group leader must run the effort. Some people are just good at solving problems, specifically technical ones. If they are willing to speak up and get the conversation going in the right direction, then let them speak. You are in the war room because the company is losing money on a serious issue that cannot be treated lightly. Jobs are at stake and customers will be lost, or at a minimum, their perception of the company will suffer. The most important advice I can give is to remain as calm as possible in the war room, and keep the activities focused. What is going to get the core issues identified and resolved? Think things through, and don't take anything personally. People become emotional in these situations and may blow up for no reason and start blaming others. You have to maintain control and make sure things move toward a resolution. If you have a group of people who are just surfing the Web, you will never get to a resolution and nothing will get done.

There is nothing better than a high-performing team in a war room. And to be a high-performing team, it takes a lot of courage to accept that you have to work longer hours than others. You have to just jump in, and get the job done. I don't understand why it seems difficult for others, and I am still surprised to see the amount of complaining that occurs in a production environment. It may not be ideal that you are working longer hours, but you will learn a lot. If you can master this technology and specialize in it, you may be surprised by the opportunities that lie ahead.

PERFORMANCE TUNING

The key to performance tuning is in knowing what change to make to get the optimal performance gain from your application. The best way to do this is by identifying the bottleneck, and continue the process until the performance is acceptable. Look at the system from a holistic approach that includes network operating system, disk virus scans, database, and whatever else you can think of that is part of the system. Identify the biggest performance impact on the system and resolve it. Then you must take a step back and re-evaluate performance. I often identify an area for improvement and the customer has laser focus on that one area. The customer generally does not understand that all I did was identify an area or a specific problem, but once that bottleneck is removed, another will surface. And often, once the immediate issue is resolved, management puts together a report saying that we found the problem and everything is fixed. The reality is that I did resolve an issue that led to poor performance, but there are additional areas on which I need to focus for the best performance. Without dedicated resources and support from management, the same situation will reoccur later on.

Becoming good at performance tuning a system takes a lot of experience with a wide variety of systems and tools. You also need to have a little luck, and above all, a desire to be good at it.

Basics

Performance tuning is taking a system that is currently in production or another environment and changing the setting and/or code for that application to get optimal performance. Given that each application is different and may use different components, it is difficult to apply one set of standards to all application components equally and expect better performance. The design patterns and how the application is used have an impact on how the system will be tuned in the production environment. Keep in mind that a setting that helped you in another situation may not be applicable when looking at a new system. You need to understand the system from a full-systems approach to be able to make effective recommendations. I have found, however, that applications that have huge performance issues are caused by a few core issues. Some applications do have more issues than working functionality. On performance-tuning engagements, I may find a few core issues that cause the majority of the performance degradation, and the customer may have reached diminishing returns or has decided that the application performs well enough for his needs, so I move on. The trick with performance tuning is to be able to conserve your efforts and make the smallest number of movements to solve solutions. Sure, if we had an infinite amount of time, we could easily start a project plan with countless number of resources to start addressing the issues. But that isn't the case.

Performance tuning of an application includes all the levels that make up the system. You can performance tune the application, the network, the databases, network, or code. Any piece of code or component can be suspect when looking into performance issues in an environment. There isn't just one tool or suite of tools that can help identify every issue. You will need to understand when to use one tool versus another. I think these factors are what make performance tuning either very rewarding or extremely frustrating. If you like challenges and have good problem-solving skills, you will be very effective at performance tuning. The challenge is that there are a lot of factors over which you don't have a lot of control. Performance tuning can take place in the production or live environments or in the load-test environments. The best practice is to performance test the changes you want to make before taking them into the production environments. There are times when you will need to make the changes directly in production, which isn't recommended, but you may not have a choice. Applications vary, based on what type of work they do; some are extremely memory-intensive, while others are I/O intensive.

Common-Denominator Approach

One of my favorite ways to determine what needs to be performance tuned when looking at the code on a system is to take the common-denominator approach. What this means is that the methods that are called the most should have the highest propriety. With the application servers of today—at least with WebLogic—you can take a look at the container and components that are deployed using JMX. You can see from a high level what are the most common EJBs, JSPs, and servlets that are used. Sort them by those that are most frequently used, and start your performance tuning there. Understand the paths that the code is taking, and put your instrumentation around this code first. The real benefit of using the common-denominator approach is that you have a systematic approach of what to start looking at first for your performance review. Taking a systematic approach can keep you on track with a methodology for performance tuning of the most critical objects. To start, get a list of the commonly used components in your applications. Look at your EJBs, controllers, and JSPs; there are ways to take a look at the container to show how often these are getting called. Identify the slow performers, and move on to the next. When you have tuned the slowest performing common denominator, you move on the next.

Bottleneck

The most common approach when it comes to performance tuning is to identify the bottleneck, solve it, and then move on to the next bottleneck. The hard part about this approach is that once the bottleneck is identified, the developers and management put all focus on this particular area and don't make headway in other areas. Put a strategy in place for identifying when you are getting diminishing returns on this performance effort, and then move on the to the next one. This can be difficult, especially helping a client with his system. It isn't easy to communicate that there may be multiple areas to the application that need work; that identifying this issue may help, but you can't be sure until you make the changes, and give it a try in an environment. This can be frustrating; it costs money with the deployment life cycle, and it costs the reputation of the business and IT organization.

When you are looking to solve a bottleneck, make sure you don't focus simply on code or performance settings. The bottleneck may be related to network, disks, operating system, firewall, application server, network appliance, or any number of other components that participate in the delivery of this application. You may have identified all the code changes and the only solution appears to be redesigning the system. This is a real problem—businesses often come to me, saying there is no option but to redesign the application. They may have had an architectural firm look at the issue, but they don't realize that an architectural firm can't offer a disk-tuning strategy. And this brings me to one of the biggest challenges in identifying the bottleneck: Specialists focus on one or more areas, and if they look at a system, they will focus attention only on the areas for which they were called. Driving the bottleneck strategy takes a generalist to first identify the area to focus attention and then bring the specialist in once it has been identified.

Validate before Making the Change

"I know what the problem is. Let me just make the change in production, and that should solve your problem." This comment is very common, and the project management team often has to control the urge to try every possible setting in production. It's important to fully understand the reason for making the change, as well as the downstream implications. Will this fix the issue, or could it make the issue worse? When in doubt, take a look at the common denominator, and see where this change fits. Will this change impact the most-used components, or is this just a tangential change that may not really give the performance boost that's expected? It takes a lot of effort to get production changes into the environment—at least, for most organization—so think through the implications, and make sure you are identifying the bottleneck and that the change will have a positive impact on one or more of the common denominators. How you determine if this will make a change is by understanding how the change will impact the applications, either in code or use of the system. This can be complicated, and in some cases, not everyone will understand how the application fits together. Changes in production and changes in the performance environment need to be validated. Once you have made the changes to the system, you can performance test the applications, take a look at the metrics, and get a picture of how this has helped or hurt the application. When you are in production, the way to do this is to make the change for one of the components in the cluster, rather than the whole cluster. For some applications, this is an all-or-nothing approach, so the only way you will know for sure is to make the change in the production domain.

One of the most common changes made in production is with allocation of threads. This is not always the right way to fix the issue, there may be a deadlock in one of the threads, or that all the threads are being consumed due to a non-responsive back-end component, and we need to investigate further. It is important to understand the cause and effect of making changes to the Java application server. The customer with this information of thread stuck usually wants to increase the number of threads, which seems to be a perfectly logical conclusion. If I went ahead with the decision to increase the threads, I might fix the issue, or make the situation even worse. It may be hard to validate all the changes, and to be honest, it takes time to understand all the relationships and dependencies among the systems. You may be the domain expert in your area, but it's most likely that you are not the domain expert in multiple areas. Get those who are experts to give input on the changes you are about to make.

Outside the Box

When you build an application you should know the application better than anyone else. When looking for performance issues, you are going to look at your components first. Without a code review there really isn't a way to know for sure if the performance bottlenecks are in your code or a dependent system. If you have reviewed your code, make sure to check the dependent systems to your applications. Thinking "outside the box" is when you need to look outside your own area of expertise to see if there are opportunities that you can tune. First, assume that you have done all the right changes in your domain and that performance can't be improved any more. Then start to look to other factors that may have caused performance issues in your application.

Less is More

Regardless of where the intended change is going to go, whether in production or any other performance environment, you need to make calculated, measurable changes in your environments. Keeping control over what you change is the only way you will know if a change has had a positive or negative effect on the performance of your application. The basic tenet is to not make a change unless there is ample evidence to show that change will improve performance of the system. You must be able to understand how this change has or could help performance. Eager to make the system perform better, I find that people are quick to make changes. There are thousands of variations of settings in an *n*-tier system; it is very difficult to say whether one change made a significant difference. When you change two or three variables at once, you won't know the impact of any one. Two could have had negative impact, and the third, considerably better impact. For example, if we change A, B, and C, then performance should increase. This is not necessarily the case. Just because a change worked for one environment, it may not increase performance in another.

When you make a change in production, you are going to know after the first big day of traffic if your change had a positive or negative impact on the performance of the system. The changes may be so small that you will be unable to detect them—that makes it tough when you have hundreds of variables to try, and you don't have a good idea of what is going to help. And if it takes a day or two to get all the changes in the environment and tested, it could be a while before you start to make a difference on the site. So when you are making changes to a site, it is very important to have some key metrics to measure your performance changes. The metrics can be the CPU-utilization memory-allocation sessions on the applications server or just reduced calls to the help desk.

When you make changes in the environments, identify some key metrics first. In general, the more EJBs and business-level work the application does, the higher the CPU load will be, while the presentations and controller components are going to be more memory-intensive. For the most part, the presentation components get and display the data retrieved from the back-end systems. They are generally more memory-intensive due to the size of the sessions. The longer your sessions, the longer they will stay around taking up space.

Out-of-the-Box Settings

With software operating systems and other applications that have tunable parameters, the vendor tries to support the greatest number of users, while generating the least number of calls to the help desk for support-related questions. Your application may fit into the standard settings, and you should not need to make modifications to the vendor's standard settings. But if you have issues with the application, or your architecture is not standard, you may want to look into the tunable parameters. The tunable parameters to Java application servers vary from how to start the virtual machine to settings that change the way the container works. Most of the configuration settings are documented, but there isn't a good way to relate the cause and effect of a setting change on another setting. The application servers are getting better at self-tuning, but for now, manual intervention must happen when your application requires additional performance or a setting change.

Very carefully consider the changes you make, as well as their impact. Companies that have problems with their application servers commonly try the "kitchen sink" approach to problem solving—they make as many changes as possible until they get it right. While this approach may work over time, it is a destructive way to go about finding the solution for your application servers' performance settings, and you may end up in a worse situation than before making any changes to the application. Consider your options before making any changes to server changes without understanding what other components it may affect.

If I have my EJBs deployed on my presentation layer, and both are using the same threads to do work, what is the implication when I increase my threads? The servlet engine will appreciate the additional threads but the EJB server may cause the CPU utilization to increase unnecessarily. When working with a vendor application, consider that he has mostly configured this application to a software component to handle 80 percent of the customers. He won't release settings that require a lot of rework and configuration—that would cost more money. Rather, consider the bottleneck and what settings would impact the bottleneck. Are you really at a point where the vendor setting needs to change? If you are unsure of the impact, get buy in from the vendor; he should be able to steer you in the right direction.

Metrics

Whenever you make decisions, either in your life or elsewhere, you probably want to reference as many sources as possible. The same holds true when looking at a complex system. The way to make educated decisions is by looking at metrics from the systems. You could get metrics on the operating systems, metrics on network utilization, metrics on disk IO, and the application itself. You need to take metrics in order to be successful at identifying the amount of time you spend doing certain functions. Be careful with metrics, though, as you may have false positives and/or environment changes, and you can't be sure that your changes made a difference. When determining the strategy for gathering your metrics, make sure that you have multiple data points, as well as control over the environmental settings that may adversely affect your results. Tools can be as simple as checking the CPU utilization on a system or looking at the network utilization. The more experience you have with the basic tools, the better chance you will have of being able to troubleshoot and identify an issue. Over time, you will gain more trust in one tool versus another and learn when to use which one. You may even consider doing some quick regression analysis to help determine if your findings are valid. The more you do this, the better you will get at quickly knowing which tool to use—sometimes, the simplest tools are the best. If you look at the applications that do performance assessments, they basically use all the tools that you can have at your fingertips. So before you start making changes find a way to identify the key variables to determine if your performance settings are making a difference. You can use metrics to determine where to spend your time.

Let's say that you spend your time working on 20 percent of the application that is getting called fifty times in a day. Say that each of those transactions takes five seconds. Compare this to another transaction that takes three seconds but is used in every call, at five thousand times per day. Which is the better part of code to work on? Logic A takes 250 seconds per day; Logic B takes 15,000 seconds per day. If you follow the model from the business—that you must have all business logic run in under four seconds—you are going to spend your time on the five-second call. In reality, the real method that is causing most of the issues is the three-second call. It isn't good enough to make a blanket statement that all business logic must be done in four seconds. This should be based on the number of times the method is called. Once you identify the number of transactions, then you can sort, based on response time. To make intelligent decisions, you need to get this data, and this can be accomplished in several ways: You can go through at a coarse, high level, and identify the interfaces. You could use a packaged application, like Perform Assure, to instrument the code. This sounds simple—all you need to do is go through the application and take some measurements. The hard part is to predict which paths the users are going to take through the system. For an existing application this should not be much a challenge, but for a new application, it can be a bit more challenging.

Baseline

Determining a baseline will help you understand the cause and effect of your changes to the system over the multiple load tests. I find that I need to take the baseline and watch the test myself; I have reservations about relying on someone else's baseline. I put a lot of trust in the baseline only when I have meticulously documented the changes and have kept diligent records of all environmental factors. This means if I run a baseline in an environment, I tear down the environment and rebuild it again the results may vary. You can assume that two baseline events have some variation. Even though you create the system exactly the same there, are things that may change. So, make sure to look at the performance increase in tests performed back to back. If you run a test on Monday and the same test on Tuesday, you may end up with results that vary. The less complex an application, however, the better chance you have the results will be consistent. The more complex applications generally show the mileage that may vary.

Tools

There are many key areas to monitor when looking at a system the application, network, disk, operating system, etc. When you are looking at the application servers, you will want to understand the resource utilization of the components deployed, such as connections pools, JMS servers, threads, and memory utilization. I usually use the tools that come with the appliance or the system-level commands that are bundled with the operating system. There are off-the-shelf products that you can use to get metrics on systems, and many customers use them to collect the data from both the operating systems and the application servers. To successfully get the data from your systems, use a tool that you are comfortable with. If you are building an application that has only a small chance of growing into a large system, there is no point in using an automated tool suite. It will take longer to set up the tools than to get the data from an available system tool.

Network

Using a command-line network tool or other monitoring tool can give you a view into the number of network connections on the box. You can also further break that down by established connections, close-waits, time-waits, and fin-waits. The settings that make the most dramatic changes to these are TCP/IP settings. You will also see they change when you change the session timeout, or if you have a lower-than-average traffic that day on the site. Using additional tools, you can further take a look at the network utilization. For the most part, you will only need to look at the network from a cursory level and the changes that impact the types of connections.

Disk

When you are performance tuning, a key indicator of what is going on in the systems is the disk check, which sees how busy the disks are when you put load on the system. When you run your load tests, keep an eye on the disks, and look for how much the disk is being used. If possible, separate your operating-system disks from your transactional disks from the logging disks. Separating the application on the disks distributes the I/O over three disks increasing performance. With the hardware disk arrays, you can really tune the system for optimal performance. I have only run into one or two places where performance tuning of the disks made a huge difference—the processes where huge batch jobs ran for a billing application. For the most part, you will have more than enough opportunities for tuning your application before you need to suspect the disks of being the bottleneck. When looking into your systems, keep the disk as always a possible reason for contention. Common convention is to separate operating-system disks from the log disk, and if possible, to have data on a different set of disks. When deploying your I/O-intensive applications consider a disk-tuning strategy. For the typical Java application, it's beneficial to have it but not necessary. This is, of course, given that you have the right resources to support and maintain the additional overhead of managing the disk appliances. If not, you can do this cost effectively by installing multiple disks, and putting the operating system on one disk, data files on another, and transactional information on a third.

There is not just one way to determine if the systems disks are the problem; having high CPU on a server does not mean that you need to make changes or upgrade your computer's chip. You must have a good understanding of what your application is doing and compare that to your disk activity. The general rule of thumb, assuming no customer I/O-intensive code, is that if you are using servlet code or presentation, you will most likely not tax the CPUs. The intensive CPU usually comes from the model layer, like EJBs. There are always exceptions to the rule, but in my experience, that is what I have found to be the case most of the time.

CPU

The CPU is a very good indicator of how much work your application servers are doing, but it can also be misleading for one simple reason: for the application server to take advantage of the CPUs on the system, it requires that you configure the application server to use more threads. The application server (at least, WebLogic) allows you to configure the threads pools up until their version, 8.x. There is a direct relationship between the number of threads you have allocated and the CPU memory and other resources you will use. Using the tools on the operating system to monitor the CPU will give you an idea of how thread-intensive the application is. Interestingly enough, an application can also show CPU utilization at a very low rate, if the application server is thread locked. Watch the server CPU on the box, and if you identify a very heavily utilized CPU, take threads dumps on the servers and look at the methods. In some cases the majority of your performance issues may be with one line of code, so check your stack traces carefully, and keep in mind that the code is using lots and lots of I/O.

Memory

There are two different ways to look at memory with the application server. The first is the physical memory on the box, and there is virtual memory. For the purpose of this section, I will limit my comments to memory available to the operating system. When you are monitoring the memory on the box, keep in mind that the physical memory you see used in the system is not the same as the Java virtual memory. So when looking at system-level memory, you will want to keep at least

20 percent available for the operating system and 80 percent for your Java virtual machines. This is a rule of thumb; it's not always the case, as you will find out when you start to test the applications.

Java

Make sure your code is written for performance. There are a lot of ways to write an application, and while it may be helpful to take classes on writing performance code, the truth is that most developers write code first, and then think about the performance later. You can check reference books that address the details of performance tuning when you've determined that the bottleneck must be related to code. When it comes to performance tuning the application server, a lot of work may need to be done before you identify the first line of code that needs to be changed. The strategy, in my opinion, should be that until you have identified the lines of code that are suspicious for the performance issues, ask yourself what the root cause is for the performance implication, and then review the code for performance issues. Most of the Java coding done in the application is business-level code that isn't that complex. A lot of the coding should be common sense—if you created an object and opened a resource, are you closing that resource and allowing the object to be marked for garbage collection? Every time you create an object, you are taking up space in the virtual machine, so come up with an object-limiting strategy, such as limiting the result sets that come back.

Java Virtual Memory

The more advanced the virtual machines get, the less and less configuration we have to do to get optimal performance on the system. The virtual machine can be configured with hundreds of different combinations. There are also a number of tools you can use to look inside the JVM to see how much memory it is using. The most common performance tuning for the Java virtual machine is adding more memory. The second most common is a setting that we call verbose garbage collection. The verbose GC will tell you how much memory is being used by the system, how much memory is free, and how frequently the Java virtual machine needs to garbage collect objects that are no longer being used. Java is an object-oriented language; you create and use objects. What better way to tune system than to not create an object? The best thing you can do is not create needless objects, such as logging in debug mode. Another way to gain performance from a system is to reuse objects that are static in nature. A lot of this is done at the code level, as it is being able to quickly identify when someone is carelessly allocating objects.

Log Levels

Extraneous logging is one of the most common performance killers an application can have. The entire organization may be jumping through hoops to tune systems and build the application infrastructure to support the application, when the problem all along could have been fixed by turning off all the logging in the application. Earlier, I mentioned conserving Java objects as much as possible, and logging is by far one of the biggest generators of extraneous objects. You might be surprised by the number of sites today with debug turned on. The thought in turning logging on is always the same: "How can we know what is happening when there is an issue if we don't have log?" A fine balance should be maintained between the amount of logging necessary to troubleshoot issues and that necessary to maintain a certain level of performance. To be fair, in some cases logging isn't the biggest bottleneck, but when you start to see diminishing returns, the logging needs to be addressed.

The debug-level logging that sends log entries to a buffered file writer is better than a non-buffered writer like "System.out.println()," but several enterprise-level applications still use the system out. The net effect of doing this is that the CPU gets a ton of I/O-related requests to store this data on the file system. And anytime you have high I/O-intensive operations, you see the CPUs increase in their activity. There will also be increased memory consumption, due to all the string objects that are created. The systems start to chew up more memory and threads until you are out of resources. And it isn't enough just to turn off the debug settings; you should check the code to make sure that the developer is checking the debug flags before sending it to the logger. It may be that you turn off logging, and your CPUs calm down, but the memory is still an issue. If this is the case, the probable cause is that you are doing your entire debug, just not putting it in a log file. In addition to checking the logging level in the application code, also check the application containers, Web servers, and database for additional logging that may have been turned on to resolve but was never turned off.

In addition to getting a performance gain by changing these settings, you will also free up the log files for the core errors that can help you identify the issue. Having clutter in a log file just makes the job of the systems administrator more difficult. Check for redundant logging of data; if you are using a Web server, you don't also need to have access logs for your application server. Check your configuration files to make sure you don't have logs that are replicated at the server and domain level. As systems get faster and disk space gets cheaper application server can handle more, but all that additional information will cost the company money in administrators' time and disk-space recovery.

I take the minimalist approach with logging. If at all possible, make sure you set your logging parameters to the lowest level possible. Keep a good rotation strategy. I keep the log files to a manageable level. Periodically check to make sure the logs are clear, and there isn't an abundance of logging. If the application is doing okay, don't worry. The management of an application is an iterative process, and having your core logging strategy in place makes the applications easier to troubleshoot when there is an issue. And you can assume it's a result of a true performance issue, rather than a configuration issue to additional logging.

EJB Issues

I once worked on issue where an EJB was deployed on a WebLogic EJB cluster. On Monday morning, we noticed the run rates on the CPUs were a lot higher than the week before—they were seventy times what they had been on Friday. The customer experienced issues on Monday morning, and the system started to slow down. The context switching (amount of times the CPU was so busy that he had to swap that request for another one) was so high that we knew something was wrong. We asked for a list of the change controls that happened over the weekend, and there was no code push. The only update was content to the system. How could a content push cause the CPUs to spike like this? The customer added an additional three hundred items to the content catalog, and in this case, the content was in a read-only entity bean. So something inside of the entity bean itself must have been causing the run queues to go so high.

Here is what happened: For the entity bean, there was one cache instance per virtual machine, and you can have a max number of one thousand cached entries before you start to passivate (save inactive data) data to disk. We quickly drew a comparison between the numbers of items. From 800 to 1100, we found our culprit. The default cache was set to 1,000 for the entity bean; we increased the cache, and the servers started working better. The content we added went from 900 entries to a little over 1,100. This little change caused the entity bean to continually try to manage the additional hundred or so of the beans in disk. This is a good example of how an out-of-the-box setting may be fine for the day when you put the application in production, but overnight, you may need to change the settings when the business changes. In this case the customer went from 800 items to 1,100 items. It is important to constantly monitor the settings of the server, and make sure you are monitoring for resources utilization.

MTU

I rarely hear people talk about the maximum transmission unit MTU when discussing application servers. This is more of a network-related setting that is done just once for the network switches. The MTU does have an impact on how we performance tune our applications. But the MTU plays a bigger role in the architectural decisions we make. The basic design is a defined packet size that everyone agrees not to exceed when sending data across the network. The Internet is set to 1,500, much larger on the local interface. On a local interface, such as 127.0.0.1, the data packets know to bypass the remote interface and go local. The advantage is that the MTU is 8k or, in some cases, 16k; this is hardware vendor-specific. We can now send a large packet, which reduces congestion on a network and improves performance. Interestingly enough, you can increase performance in a system by the technical layout of the application and you may even be able to increase performance by just changing network settings. These are some of the areas in which you can be at a disadvantage if you are a specialist in the application server space, but you don't understand how networks work. You can learn about these settings, though, by keeping aware of the issues that come up in your environment or working through them yourself.

An example of this happened on a customer site that had poor response times on the servers. The response time just wasn't what was anticipated; the request was taking 105 seconds to complete versus the 30 seconds on the developer's laptop. The developer who built the application insisted this was a server issue, and the application worked fine locally. I didn't get to spend a lot of time investigating this particular issue, but I assumed that the proxy servers were enabled. At this point, it was anyone's guess why these local clients were so much slower than the developer's machines.

They began comparing the computers and the hardware memory. Why would one client's computer work so much faster than the other's? This didn't seem to make any sense. They finally noticed a daemon that was running on the developer's machine that was not on the client's machine. As part of any good troubleshooting exercise, make the environments equal so they shut down the daemon process. The developer's machine was just as slow as the client's machine. The daemon was a network-compression utility that made communication over a virtual private network (VPN) much faster by removing the headers before sending the data. You sometimes never know what is going to help an application perform better. You really need to be observant in the environments, and look out for subtle changes in the system. This is where breadth of knowledge is helpful rather than having a specialization. It doesn't matter how much you know about software development, these issues are system-related. As just shown, network and client software can have an impact on the application. You can make these changes in a closed environment, but be careful when you are deploying applications for external customers. You will run into unexpected results if you do this in a Web-based environment.

Session Management

Let's say you have an external-facing application designed to serve hundreds of thousands of users. The business requirement is to have the customer-session information persist for twelve hours with a session size of about five megabytes. Setting the session timeout on the server to twelve hours with a five-megabyte session size can lead to issues. If you do not have enough memory to store all those sessions in memory, you will often get an OutOfMemory error when the session gets to a certain level on the servers. Servers will start crashing or just need to be recycled. This problem is a configuration issue and can be solved in a couple of ways: you can solve this through code, by reducing the size of the session; you can solve this by decreasing the session timeout, or you can fix this by adding more application servers. I think when you are open about the issues the customer will be open to the solutions. This may take some positioning, but it isn't difficult to get the point across. The simplest solution is to change the session timeout to half of what it was or to some number less than the current, where you can handle the number of sessions without issue. You can have your session last for twelve hours, and you won't crash if you have fifty instances versus five. Then explain the various solutions. Solutions A is a code change and requires a complete regression test. Solution B is going to cost the change control and time to implement. And Solution C is going to require adding additional resources and cost to the applications. When you position the alternatives, the customer will usually see that he can live with a reduced session timeout, rather than having to deal with the other two options.

People are used to the Internet, and they know that if they do not get the work done in that session, it is going to expire. It's in your best interests to help manage expectations and keep the site running. There are always some exceptions, but keep that in mind when making the configuration settings.

Web Servers

Using a Web server in your application can help the performance of your system, but it can also hurt the performance. Knowing when to use the Web server varies on a case-by-case basis. Depending on the application architecture, there will be some situations where you need to have a Web server and others where you will not. For the most part, a Web server will always be cheaper to operate than an application server. The big difference is that the Web server serves static content, whereas the application server has dependent systems. I like to use a Web server to hand off all static requests and keep away from the application server.

The Web servers are just as capable of producing poor results in production as any other component. The Web servers are susceptible to operating-system server settings, image size, and a host of other issues that might seem unrelated. The Web servers can also be tuned, keep this in mind the next time a Web server request is taking longer than expected. What are the symptoms, and can you fix this with a configuration setting. Have you checked the log files? This could be an issue related to a configuration file. Anything that is static could be served by the Web servers; this includes HTML files, CSS file images, and anything else you would want to offload from the application server. In general, you want to keep the application server focused on the dynamic content. If you have an application that has a lot of images and static content, you will really like this approach and should see a performance benefit from doing this. There may be a performance hit if you don't have a lot of images with the additional layer, so there is a trade-off. And without doing some testing, you will never know if the Web server increases or decreases performance.

In addition to using the Web server for static content, I also encourage using proxy servers to proxy requests to the application servers. This topic of proposing one solution versus the other is often debated. There are those who always want to use hardware, whenever possible, and I doubt I could convince them otherwise. With the technologies today, I think it makes some sense to hand off the affinity to the Web, and use application servers to handle the session information.

Using a proxy server, such as the WebLogic proxy plug-in in front of WebLogic, will require more maintenance. It might not always give you the best performance boost, if your application doesn't have a lot of images. The proxy plug-in only routes http requests. It can route your T3 request or RMI, but this refers to about 80 percent of Web applications—only those have a presentation layer. Using the Web server plug-in allows you to throttle requests from the Web servers. Handling the reroutes at this Web-server level gives the application administrators more control over their domain, whereas the network teams may be responsible for the hardware. These requests can very easily be rerouted, or you can shut down requests altogether by putting up a splash page to redirect traffic, if needed. Now, the maintenance of the site gets easier. You aren't worried about those who try to hit the servers when you are trying to bring up clusters. When you bring up the clusters, a server will inevitably come up first, unless you adopt an automated way to bring up the servers. Then you may still have one that comes up first, but this first server will now try to handle the entire request that comes through to it. This is an issue, because the Web farm was designed to handle all of the requests, and you only have one server now. With the Web servers in front, you can wait until the farm is back online.

Performance Recommendations

Before you start giving too many recommendations, remember to use your words wisely. Customers are looking for a setting or one-click fix to get the performance out of their systems. They may have been through some troubleshooting with a support organization and assume they have tried everything. The customers' most common reaction to a poorly performing application is to increase the threads without understanding the overall impact to the application. Or they add more resources to the application, which can also impact performance. In some cases, the number of changes the customer has made makes the job of getting the system back on track much harder. A common misconception with Java application servers is that if we give it more resources, the application will perform better. The most common issue with application servers is threads. When an application requires them, you need to make sure they exist. The ratio of threads to applications is really the key. A common mistake is to add more threads to fix a problem, when the real issue was memory consumption. The additional threads consume additional memory; now the application will crash much quicker. Performance testing tries to see if the application can handle the projected load based on a time interval. Performance tuning takes on many forms and iterations. You should consider several key factors when you take part in a performance objective. Never assume that someone knows everything about performance tuning, just because he is leading the effort. He usually will appreciate helpful ideas that are grounded in reality. If you are new to performance tuning, keep your ideas to yourself. Observe what is happening before commenting. Prove your ideas before recommending them.

Coarse-Grained/Fine-Grained

We cannot ignore the application design—how the system was designed. A helpful way to look at this is how the application is getting the data from the back-end components. Fine-grained design patterns are used for the low-level design of the application. Some architectural patterns comprise multiple design patterns to provide an enterprise design methodology. A simple example of this is to imagine that you are going out to lunch and need ten dollars for a meal. You go the ATM, get ten dollars, and purchase your lunch; this is the coarse-grained example. The fine-grained example would be if you went to the ATM, got a dollar, got in line, and ordered your food. The person behind the counter then tells you that you need nine more dollars, so you get in your car, go to the ATM, and get another dollar. Now the person at the counter says you need eight more dollars. This process continues until you have gone back and forth the ATM to get the full ten dollars.

Think about the implication of the coarse-grained approach versus the fine-grained approach. With coarse-grained approach, you know what you will need to complete the transaction of purchasing your lunch. The fine-grained access is to get bits and pieces of data—and you also need to be careful not to start a transaction before you have all the necessary data to finish the transaction. Going back to get another piece of data in the middle of a transaction will cause unnecessary wait times in line.

When you look at a J2EE application, you see the many different components you can use, and the choices seem overwhelming. For the most part unless you are writing completely custom applications, you will need to understand the patterns in details. If you are writing a business application, you will use a framework that was built using patterns. You will only need to use a few of the design patterns to solve specific challenges. Rely on frameworks when developing your applications. There will be additional challenges as the integration needs of the application increase. Keep that in mind when designing your systems.

SUMMARY

High-Performance Applications

Java technology has advanced to the point where applications can perform almost as fast as code that is compiled native to an operating system. This has been achieved by optimized Java virtual machines that cache frequently, use classes, and other optimized algorithms. When designing, developing, and supporting these applications, you should have a high-performance application. The key to having a high-performing application is to conserve as much energy as you can and make as few steps as possible. Having a high-performing application starts with a good design and sound performance strategy. You must be ready to work through the issues as they come up. There really is no reason why every application could not be a high-performing application. It doesn't come overnight and certainly not without putting the resources into making it happen. To build the high-performance application, it will take a consistent strategy that identifies the issues and resolves them. When you look at this from a practical perspective, it is relatively simple. If you are able to solve all the technical challenges as you run into them, you will have a high-performing application. The difference between the high-performing application and the average application is that there is not a systematic approach to making the product perform better. You may have used all the right design patterns and hired good engineers, but things do not always go the way you plan. It is easy to code for the predictable path. The hardest part is to know the exceptions you may encounter after the code is written and running. The high-performing applications have ownership built into the applications, and management needs to buy in, that they want to have high-performing applications. You can do this organically; it isn't common to have the organic approach work, especially when the company is doing what it can to limit the resources put into the project.

Keys to Success

After reading about all the issues that companies have, you may ask, "Why try it?" It does not seem possible to get a system up and running properly. As a matter of fact, I have saved the jobs of many people by identifying and controlling the issues they are facing. The concepts are not overly complex, but there are a lot of places to look when managing a system. You must know which steps to take to gain system stability. If you are taking an application to production, you must be aware of the things you need before making the move. You can make several tactical changes to get a system up and running. These require skill and commitment from the management to support those who are interested in making the changes. You also must adopt a process that supports creativity and, ultimately, get the best application to market. I hope you have a better understanding of what I feel are the key areas of focus when setting up your *n*-tier applications.

Where to Focus Time

Determining where to spend your time working on an application is difficult. I think it is best to break down the application by core business functionality. Focus your attention on the areas that are of most importance to the business. At the end of the day, you need to make sure the business needs are met. I think this is where technologists run into trouble. From a technical perspective, we want to solve the challenging technical problems, and that is why we are good at what we do. The challenge is that what is best for the business isn't always what we want to do. Learning how to take a step back and get an idea of where you need to focus your time can be hard, but it is necessary if you want to change the systems. When trying to determine where to spend your time keep in mind that the predicted path may not be the same as the actual. In reality, it is completely different. Be prepared to be flexible, and if you are focusing on an area that is not going to give you the performance improvement, it is okay to take a step back and focus attention on other, more lucrative areas. There is a reason the application is not working as expected. There is a technical reason why the application is failing. And you have all the tools at your disposal. You just need to know where to look and which tool to use.

Performance Factors

Building and deploying an application is only the beginning for the long journey of the business application. The business application is in a constant state of flux, and only when you look at the application from a holistic approach and understand all the interdependencies between the applications and their environment will you start to understand how the performance tuning works. There are lots of switches and flags that you can set on your servers' operating system, but the key is to know which flags and switches to set for your application.

You might ask, "If we designed the application better, would we have needed these switches in the first place?" Becoming good at performance-engineering factors requires the ability to look beyond the immediate symptoms to be able to pull from past experiences and apply that to the situation at hand. Ask yourself, "What are some of the similarities between what I am seeing today and what I have seen in the past?" It is your job to get the experiences that will take the business applications to the next level of performance. And to do that, you need understanding and clarity, not from a fine-grained level but from a higher, twenty-thousand-foot level. And be ready to dive deep into any one of many vertical areas to find the solutions.

The Right Engineer

A well-rounded engineer can solve the issues and help transition that knowledge to others. The right engineer is the one who everyone gives glowing recommendations to and says, "What would this company be without him?" Companies are full of people trying to sabotage others' efforts. They don't feel as valuable if they give up information. Imagine what a company could do if it had a culture of everyone contributing at the same level. What could your company do if everyone was the right engineer who wanted the process to succeed? Your business or corporate culture may be the reason your corporate applications are not as successful as the can be. Fear of layoffs, outsourcing, and lack of commitment to the employees brings self-doubt. Engineers wonder why anyone should benefit from their work, or why they took the time in their off-hours to develop resolutions to issues.

You may not get noticed for your efforts but that's okay if you consider the benefits beyond this position. Your career is composed of several critical steps. Company politics aside, my challenge to the engineer is, "Do you want to be the person who just got by? Or do you want to be someone substantial?" When I talk about being substantial, I mean someone who could save a company millions of dollars a year—this could go on your résumé, not that you hoarded knowledge or became apathetic after being passed up for promotions. I know there are people who think their job is "just a job," but I don't know how to relate to those people. Wouldn't it be nice to succeed for yourself and have the satisfaction that you did a good job?

Closing Thoughts

It's not impossible to build robust enterprise applications that truly help a business process and add value to the company, but they do require a strong understanding of how the elements fit together in our domains. You also need to have a solid understanding of the components and how they work and integrate together. You then must focus your effort on working on the relationships between the various systems. These relationships include system relationships, people relationships, and even your relationships with your peers, which allow you to successfully implement the technical solutions in an ever-changing business environment. The more I work with the Java application server, the more confident I am that the limitations in technology will be overcome, and this will be the foundation for our enterprises, now and well into the future.

Today's applications and platforms are built on sophisticated technologies. Companies that discover how to successfully implement these technologies are those that can reduce operational expense and increase productivity. In a number of instances, the case for giving up the technology is cost-related, but I feel that the main reason behind the surrender of technology is that the company does not understand the technology or how to implement it in a cost-effective way.

I hope that you have enjoyed reading *Affinity* and learning about the complex relationships between the Java application server and the enterprise. As the technologies mature the frameworks and tools develop you will find that building robust applications is getting easier. Good luck implementing your Java application servers.

THE END

REFERENCES

Philip J Gill. *Strategies for Distributed Systems?* http://www.strategicfocus.com/ Two%20Tiers%20Or%20Three1998.htm [viewed 5/07/2007]

Brian Pontarelli, JavaWorld.com (07/26/04). *J2EE security: Container versus custom.* http://www.javaworld.com/javaworld/jw-07-2004/jw-0726-security.html [viewed]

Alan Baumgarten (01/16/2004). *J2EE Design Patterns.* http://dev2dev.bea.com/ pub/a/2004/01/baumgarten.html [viewed]

Vijay S. Ramachandran (12/2001). *Design Patterns for Optimizing the Performance of J2EE Applications.* http://java.sun.com/developer/technicalArticles/ J2EE/J2EEpatterns/ [viewed]

Sun Microsystems (1994–2007). *J2EE v1.4 Specification.* http://java.sun.com/ j2ee/1.4/docs/#specs [viewed]

Sun Microsystems (2002). *J2EE Patterns Catalog.* http://java.sun.com/blueprints/ patterns/catalog.htm [viewed]

Index

978-0-595-45626-0
0-595-45626-X

www.ingramcontent.com/pod-product-compliance
Lightning Source LLC
Chambersburg PA
CBHW071153050326
40689CB00011B/2089